The Listening Heart

Brother Ramon SSF is an Anglican Franciscan friar, and one of today's most popular writers on spirituality. For the last six years he has followed a call to a hermit lifestyle.

His numerous books include *Franciscan Spirituality*, *The Way of Love* and *The Heart of Prayer*.

Also available by the same author
from Marshall Pickering

THE WAY OF LOVE
Following Christ through Lent to Easter

THE HEART OF PRAYER
Finding a time, a place and a way to pray

The Listening Heart

Seven Days with the Seven Churches of the Apocalypse

BROTHER RAMON SSF

Illustrations by Molly Dowell

Marshall Pickering
An Imprint of HarperCollinsPublishers

Marshall Pickering is an Imprint of
HarperCollins*Religious*
Part of HarperCollins*Publishers*
77–85 Fulham Palace Road, London W6 8JB

First published in Great Britain
in 1996 by Marshall Pickering

1 3 5 7 9 10 8 6 4 2

A catalogue record for this book is
available from the British Library

0 551 03050 X

Typeset by Harper Phototypesetters Ltd, Northampton
Printed and bound in Great Britain by
Caledonian International Book Manufacturing Ltd, Glasgow

Contents

Preface: Geared Up for Retreat   1

Introduction: The Risen Christ in Glory (Revelation 1:9–20) 10

1 *Spent Enthusiasm*: The Church at Ephesus (2:1–7)   28
    Morning: Orthodox and Energetic   33
    Evening: Losing Your First Love   39
2 *Persecution and Glory*: The Church at Smyrna (2:8–11)   48
    Morning: Christ Who was Dead and is Alive   54
    Evening: The Crown of Life   61
3 *The Throne of Satan*: The Church at Pergamum
    (2:12–17)   72
    Morning: Martyrdom and Heresy   77
    Evening: Christ's Two-edged Sword   83
4 *The Danger of Compromise*: The Church at Thyatira
    (2:18–29)   92
    Morning: A Corrupted Faith   96
    Evening: Hold Fast!   102
5 *Dead or Alive?*: The Church at Sardis (3:1–6)   112
    Morning: Professing not Possessing   115
    Evening: The Faithful Few   121

6 *Love and Faithfulness*: The Church at Philadelphia
(3:7–13)   128
    Morning: An Open Door   132
    Evening: 'I have loved you ... I will keep you' 137
7 *Tepid and Nauseous*: The Church at Laodicea (3:14–22)   146
    Morning: The Judging Christ   149
    Evening: Patient, Waiting Saviour   157

Epilogue: The Listening Heart   169

The Seven Churches of Asia Minor

Geared Up for Retreat

This book is prepared for the Christian who feels the need for a retreat* and who is willing to be confronted with the Risen Christ. Such a retreat may be planned in your own home, away alone, or with a friend in a holiday caravan or cottage, or taking the book for a retreat to a retreat house or monastery, while sharing in the daily worship of the community. It may also be taken up by a group and used in the context of a retreat or as a series of devotional studies on a daily or weekly basis, provided that as much time is given to prayer and silence as to study and reading. This is not a book to be 'read through' but to be savoured in the presence of Christ, and it will make no sense to read the text of the book without the prayerful perusal of the appropriate Bible passage.

*Guidance on various approaches and information on retreats may be found in Brother Ramon's books *Deeper into God, Heaven on Earth* and *The Heart of Prayer*. Contemporary information, addresses and themes of retreats and retreat houses may be obtained from The National Retreat Association, The Central Hall, 256 Bermondsey Street, London SE1 3UJ.

HOW TO USE THE BOOK

The Biblical text is taken from the **Book of Revelation** (otherwise referred to as **The Apocalypse**), chapters one to three, and there are two sections for each day of the week — morning and evening. The morning section consists of a word of *teaching* from the Risen Christ to his *Church*, with a meditation on the scripture, a prayer and response.

The evening section consists of a word of personal *devotion* from the Risen Christ to the *believer* — an application of the meaning of the passage, with its appropriate meditation, prayer and response.

Don't be afraid of the word *teaching*. In this book it communicates something of the nature and character of the Christ who is our Lord and Saviour, with the implications of what it means to live in him and to follow him. We shall not only 'read his letter' to us as Church and believer, but if we enter into the spirit of the book we shall apply our listening heart to what the Holy Spirit is saying. Receptive stillness leads to listening, listening leads to experience, and experience leads to a mingling of the mind and will of Christ with the mind and heart of the believer.

The retreatant must expect a word of judgement and a word of mercy, for it is a two-edged sword of flaming love that flashes from the mouth of Christ. We shall find ourselves at one moment on our faces before the Lord and Judge of all, and at the next moment lying enfolded in the arms of compassion, filled with joy, perhaps accompanied by tears.

THE DAILY PATTERN

This depends on the way, you, the reader use the book, and as retreatant you will have to work out your own specific details depending on where you are, but the following timetable is given for guidance:

7.00 a.m.	Rise, ablutions
7.30 a.m.	Psalm and meditation (or Order of Morning Prayer)
8.00 a.m.	Breakfast
9.00 a.m.	Morning theme: This unit includes the *centering down* method described below and use of the appropriate section in the retreat book
10.30 a.m.	Exercise (walk, etc.)
12.00 noon	Meal preparation, cooking, eating, rest
2.00 p.m.	Manual/creative work (your own choice, e.g. carpentry, embroidery, gardening, painting, bookbinding, calligraphy, writing, etc.)
4.30 p.m.	Pot of tea
5.00 p.m.	Evening theme (as Morning theme)
6.30 p.m.	Exercise (walk, etc.)
7.00 p.m.	Light supper
7.30 p.m.	Psalm and meditation (or Order of Evening Prayer)
8.00 p.m.	Music (listening or making); reflection on the day; journal writing
9.30 p.m.	Compline and retire

Some retreatants will be able to 'sit' for an hour or more, while beginners may prefer to take the book's themes into a meditative walk.

3

DIET

The matter of diet may be settled by the provisions in a retreat house, but the Middle-Eastern vegetarian recipes included may enhance the whole retreat if they appeal to you. Why not try them out beforehand?

These simple vegetarian meals for each of the seven days are from the region of Asia Minor, which includes the seven churches of the text (present-day Turkey). These meals are neither exotic nor gourmet, but provide a simple and basic meal which is easily prepared with a minimum of fuss. The retreat should cultivate an attitude of quiet thoughtfulness (called *mindfulness*) while preparing, cooking, eating and digesting the food. When you eat, eat; when you walk, walk; when you sleep, sleep. Simplicity, concentration, single-mindedness – all with no strain or pretence.

Do not under-estimate the value of such an exercise. The peeling of an onion, the chopping of a carrot, may be the moment of insight into the interdependence of all living beings within the natural order. This may be the glimpse of cosmic awareness which will transform your way of seeing and of living. The recipes are, of course, voluntary, and amounts may vary according to appetite!

CENTERING DOWN

This is a simple method in preparation for the daily meditation for both morning and evening. If you have your own method then use it, but if not, this method will help you. There are three steps: 1. Resting; 2. Breathing; 3. Opening.

1. Resting. Go to your prayer place; loosen all tight clothing, removing footgear; find your own posture (lying, sitting, prayer stool); let go all tension in physical relaxation, stretching and relaxing each part of your body, beginning with the soles of your feet and slowly moving upwards to the crown of your head – until you are relaxed in body and yet alert in mind. Find your centre of stillness in God.

2. Breathing. The second step consists of a simple breathing exercise to bring your respiration into a slightly slower and deeper mode than usual, leading to the breathing of a prayerful longing for God.

First, don't *change* your breathing, but simply *note* its rate and rhythm. Now gently begin to breathe from the diaphragm instead of from the top of the chest (belly-breathing), and with the deepening slow it down slightly. Your tummy will rise as you begin such breathing, and as the tops of your lungs fill, it will lower slightly. After a minute or two of such easy, relaxed breathing, find your own level – that is, a level that suits you without strain or effort. The aim here is to let go all stress and be completely relaxed. No push or effort, but simple, easy, passive resting in God.

3. Opening. You are already open to God, but this word *opening* now indicates your receptiveness to the theme of the session. It is the bridge period between the breathing exercise of resting in God, and entering into the meditation which brings you his inspiration and illumination. Stay with this opening attitude until you feel ready to begin the appropriate session with the scripture reading.

This *centering down* exercise should be practised at the beginning of each morning and evening session.

DAILY ELEMENTS

The elements of the morning and evening sessions, with their themes, are therefore:

a Centering down
b Prayerful reading of the appropriate scripture passage
c Perusal of the meditative material
d Slow repetition of the prayer provided
e Period of silence
f Response

The retreatant is free to incorporate other liturgical or devotional material around the theme, such as sharing in the eucharist if staying in or near a monastic house. But this book does not presume any more than the above.

SHOPPING FOR THE RETREAT

The following list is suggested (with your own extras or alternatives) if you intend using the recipes included for each day:

• Mixed dried beans
• Chick peas (or 1 tin)
• 2 lbs courgettes

- 3 lbs ripe tomatoes
- 1 tube tomato concentrate
- Vegetable stock cubes
- Oil for cooking
- Olive oil
- Small pasta (i.e. small cut macaroni)
- 2 green peppers; 2 aubergines; 2 carrots; 1 large leek
- 3 lbs onions
- 1 lb broccoli florets
- 1 carton natural yoghurt
- 1 lemon; celery; ½ cucumber
- Potatoes
- Eggs
- Cheshire or feta cheese for crumbling
- Hard cheese for grating
- 2 lbs runner or french beans
- Dried mixed herbs, plus marjoram, cumin
- Fresh herbs – mint and parsley
- Vinegar, salt
- 1 lb flour (wholemeal or plain white)
- Bread
- 4 ozs patna or basmati rice

SO BEGIN

We are now ready to read the Introduction, which sets the tone and context of the seven daily themes, and this will involve reading the whole of the first chapter of the book of Revelation.

So do that now!

Pantocrator: 'I Am the Alpha and the Omega'.

The Risen Christ in Glory
Revelation 1:9–20

I, John, your brother who share with you in Jesus the persecution and the kingdom and the patient endurance, was on the island called Patmos because of the word of God and the testimony of Jesus. I was in the Spirit on the Lord's day, and I heard behind me a loud voice like a trumpet saying, 'Write in a book what you see, and send it to the seven churches, to Ephesus, to Smyrna, to Pergamum, to Thyatira, to Sardis, to Philadelphia, and to Laodicea.'

Then I turned to see whose voice it was that spoke to me, and on turning I saw seven golden lampstands, and in the midst of the lampstands I saw one like the Son of Man, clothed with a long robe and with a golden sash across his chest. His head and his hair were white as white wool, white as snow; his eyes were like a flame of fire, his feet were like burnished bronze, refined as in a furnace, and his voice was like the sound of many waters. In his right hand he held seven stars, and from his mouth came a sharp, two-edged sword, and his face was like the sun shining with full force.

When I saw him, I fell at his feet as though dead. But he placed his right hand on me, saying, 'Do not be afraid; I am the first and the last, and the living one. I was dead, and see, I am alive for ever and ever; and I have the keys of Death and of Hades. Now write what you have seen, what is, and what is to take place after this. As for the mystery of the seven stars that you saw in my right hand, and the seven golden lampstands: the seven stars are the angels of the seven churches, and the seven lampstands are the seven churches.

The Risen Christ in Glory

PATMOS AND THE SEVEN CHURCHES

The Church and the Christian encounter the living God in scripture. Before we hear the word of God to *us* in these chapters we must first understand that it was a word to a specific church at a specific time, dealing with judgement and glory, persecution, suffering and the experience of grace *then and there*.

We must be careful about a literal interpretation of this apocalyptic book, but we shall find that the Holy Spirit will take the *then and there* words of the text and translate them into the *here and now* for us.

As we meditate, this will in turn be translated into the *there and then* of the future. For Christ, the Alpha and Omega, will place our feet upon the path that he alone knows, and in which we can trust him to lead us gently and firmly, for he is 'the same yesterday, today and for ever'.

Patmos is a rocky island in the Mediterranean Sea, one of a group, forty miles off the coast of Asia Minor. It was the first and last call on the journey from Rome to Ephesus. Its shape is a crescent, ten miles long by five miles wide, and a place of banishment for political prisoners.

Christians were regarded as criminals, and St John the Divine, as we have come to know him, was an apostolic leader, caught up in the Roman persecution against Christ and his Church.

He was banished to the island of Patmos, working in the quarries there with insufficient food and scantily clad. He was probably beaten, though confinement may have been sporadic because the island was surrounded by a dangerous sea and escape was unlikely.

The beautiful Greek word for sea, *thalassa*, is found twenty-five times in the Apocalypse, and the voice of Christ is as the sound of many waters (1:15) resounding through the book.

The Seven Churches are found in a rough circle, beginning with Ephesus, through the cities named in order of Smyrna, Pergamum, Thyatira, Sardis, Philadelphia, Laodicea and back to Ephesus – like a necklace. The divine, or complete, number is seven, and this mystic number runs right through the Apocalypse.

These seven symbolize the whole Church, not only in that time of persecution when the Apocalypse was read secretly throughout the persecuted churches, but down through the ages to our own day. Persecution and martyrdom will persist through time, and if the Church of God was more faithful to God in our own day it would be persecuted, not respectably courted by hypocrites without and within. The faithful Church will be the arena of God's judgement and mercy until he carries his people home to the eternal kingdom of the last chapters of the book of the Revelation.

LETTERS FROM THE RISEN CHRIST

We shall be reading letters which were written long ago and far away, but they will become startlingly real to us, just as a letter from a beloved brings the presence close to the lover. But we are not simply the recipients of a letter, and it would be sad if we treated these letters, or the Bible as a whole, as a written document from afar. We should then be dealing with the dead letter instead of with the living Spirit (2 Corinthians 3:6). And how absurd it would be for a lover to be engrossed in a love letter when the beloved was by his side, longing to enter into the communion of love – while he was only interested in the literary composition, however beautiful!

Christ himself comes to us through his word, and his presence is mediated through these letters. He comes to us both as the Almighty (*Pantocrator*) and as the Beloved. We shall be scorched by his love and seared by his judgement – both are essential, for we are not involved in a sentimental devotional exercise, but caught up in a relationship in which we are confronted with the divine Love. 'It is a fearful thing to fall into the hands of the living God', for 'our God is a consuming fire' (Hebrews 10:31; 12:29).

We are all on the same pilgrimage of love, but our life stories and lifestyles are all different. You must bring your actual workaday life under the scrutiny of the words before us in our text. I have been a Christian in the market-place world of work, then as an undergraduate and graduate, going on to ordination and work as parish priest and university chaplain. From there I joined the Anglican Franciscan Order (SSF), and became involved in preaching, teaching, missions, retreats and counselling. Then after a time as Guardian of our monastery at Glasshampton I went off to explore the hermit life, and am well into the seventh year of such exploration. This is my story, not yours, but you have your own equally valid story. I reflect on my path in the light of the themes in this book – you will find light shining on your path, for we minister to one another within the Body of Christ.

THE ANGELS OF THE SEVEN CHURCHES

The letters are addressed to the angels of the churches, and we have to ask ourselves who they are. It is best to hold before us the various responses which have been given to their identity, for they all have something to contribute in our understanding of the text.

1. It has been thought that *angelos* (messenger) here means the pastor, teacher, representative or presbyter of the church in question. It may be that John called them together, or directed the letters to them to carry back to the churches. But *angelos* almost always means an angelic being in the New Testament.

2. When we read of a bishop in the writings immediately outside the New Testament we must remember that the monarchic bishops had not yet developed, so that Timothy may be thought of as the presbyter-bishop of Ephesus, or Archippus of Laodicea. But the above objection also applies to these.

3. The letters themselves indicate that the 'angel' partakes of the character and destiny of the church far beyond that of

any mortal messenger; so that a 'guardian angel' may be meant. In Old Testament thinking there were such angels who were guardians over nations, communities and individuals (see Daniel 10:13, 20). This is carried over into the New Testament where Jesus refers to the guardian angels of children in Matthew 18:10, and Peter's guardian angel is part of the story in Acts 12:16. The difficulty here is that the angel is rebuked sometimes for the sins of the church — though Origen believed that it was the angel's responsibility!

4. Then there is the Hebrew and Greek idea that earthly things have a heavenly counterpart or ideal, and that one presbyter, or a group of them, is addressed in an 'ideal' manner, or that the symbolical ideal is that of the church itself 'as it ought to be'.

There is no need for us to dogmatize about the interpretations but to bear in mind these possibilities, after all, the application of scripture to our situation has many levels. Certainly the angel is bound to the church, and there is a sense in which we all bear angel-responsibility as messengers and representatives of our churches and of our Lord. So perhaps we should take the message to our own hearts, our own churches, both in judgement and in mercy.

PANTOCRATOR:
RISEN, OMNIPOTENT AND MERCIFUL

The immediate context of the letters to the seven churches is set within the vision that John the Divine has of the Risen Christ, particularly in Revelation 1:9–20, where the word

Pantocrator is first used. It is used throughout the Apocalypse, and affirms the deity of Christ: 'I am the Alpha and the Omega ... who is and who was and who is to come, the Almighty (*Pantocrator*)' (1:8).

I have before me as I write one of the great Orthodox icons of the Pantocrator. Around the radiant and illumined head of the Risen Christ are the symbolic letters of his divinity. It is a strange and powerful icon, and I have kept it with me over the last twelve years, since the first six-month experiment of the hermit life. Solitude on the edge of the Lleyn Peninsula opposite the island of Bardsey, with the wild and crashing sea below, could not have been too different from John's experience on the island of Patmos.

If I look straight into the face of the Pantocrator Christ I see complete integrity, transparency, searching judgement. If I half-close my eyes, the whole face takes on a more gentle mien. The eyes become compassionate, radiant light suffuses the features, and the hand of blessing is lifted in healing and forgiveness. We shall find these two elements of judgement and grace intermingling through our readings. But always we shall find that the judgement which is expressed in the word and character of Christ, if followed humbly and honestly, leads to the divine Love in which all judgement is contained.

TRANSCENDENCE AND IMMANENCE

One thing we must be careful about in approaching the Apocalypse is that in such books the transcendence of God is upfront, as if to assure the persecuted believers that the might of the Roman Emperor is but temporal and mortal, but the power of Christ is that of the sovereign Pantocrator who holds all things in his hand. This is the transcendent revelation of apocalyptic theology, but we must remember that this is but part of the revelation of God in Christ. We must also hold within our mind and experience the immanence of God.

God is transcendent, above and beyond this world of time and space, but he is also immanent, dwelling at the heart of the created order. The very breath which we breathe, the spring sap which rises in the trees, the creative pulse which causes the sun to rise and set, the moon to wax and wane, the seas to ebb and flow – this is a manifestation of the immanence of God. In other words, of the Holy Spirit, the Lord and Lifegiver. The more we become aware of the dynamic life within the communion of the Holy Trinity, the more we shall understand the experience of both the transcendence and the immanence of God.

As I write these words they are set within a day in which I spend some hours digging and caring for the monastery vegetable garden, and that involves me in meditation of the divine indwelling in nature. It not only possesses me in the inwardness of my own spirituality, but is in the very earth which I turn over with my spade. I pierce the earth in order to plant seed potatoes. The awareness of sun, moisture and warm air makes me reflect upon the creative womb of the earth which will nurture the buried seed until it germinates, bursts forth above the ground and reaches up towards sun, sky and the bearing of fruit. I am also aware of the masculine and feminine analogies implicit in all this co-operative activity, and the whole wonder of the immanence of God brings me close to tears. And running alongside this as a sort of counterpoint in parallel and complement is the appearance of the Pantocrator in the Apocalypse.

If I trembled in wonder, gentleness and tears at the experience of God's immanence, I am now confronted with his transcendence – the God who is and who was and who is to come, the Almighty.

There is no contradiction here, though there is certainly profound paradox, for the prophetic and the mystical experiences of God are both grounded in scripture and in theological experience. Prophets and mystics each belong to the revelation of God's judgement and mercy.

The God who confronts me in mighty power is the Risen One who has conquered death and hell, and he causes me to tremble in recognition. For in his judgement he calls into question all the darkness, sinfulness and denials of love which have run through my whole life. If he were exclusively power, majesty, purity, judgement I would need to tremble; not simply in awe, but in a certain fear, for his two-edged sword would split asunder all my evasions, hypocrisy, malice and self-justification. There would be no place for me to hide, and I would have no garment to cover my naked need. Because I know that his judgement is contained within his love I am able to stand humbly yet lovingly before him.

The word *Pantocrator* is very different from the great god Pan. *Pan* means all-embracing – a sort of pagan deity who does not differentiate between good and evil, or whose immanence is one of fertility and sensuality. There is a great deal of morally neutral and natural wisdom to be learned from positive nature mysticism, which holds natural life-force and moral righteousness in active and healthy tension, but there is also a warning note to be sounded.

There have always been nature and fertility cults which look back to the kind of Canaanite religion of the Old Testament and run right through to some of the darker New Age teachings which divorce nature mysticism from holy righteousness. The great monotheistic faiths all warn against a natural religion which is divorced from justice and moral law. A 'mystical sense' which is simply based on natural feeling could well be an expression of fallen human nature cloaking itself in pseudo-religion which avoids issues of truth and compassion based in righteousness.

Israel was constantly falling into such paganism – the kind of religion which was full of lip service without the heart, full of blood sacrifices without compassion, full of ritualistic and priest-ridden ceremonies which cloaked injustice, oppression and sexual deviation. The prophetic word sounds loud and clear against such practices:

> *I cannot endure solemn assemblies with iniquity.*
> *Your new moons and your appointed festivals my soul hates;*
> *they have become a burden to me. I am weary of bearing them.*
> *When you stretch out your hands, I will hide my eyes from you;*
> *even though you make many prayers, I will not listen; your*
>   *hands are full of blood.*
> *Wash yourselves; make yourselves clean; remove the evil of your*
>   *doings from before my eyes;*
> *cease to do evil, learn to do good;*
> *seek justice, rescue the oppressed,*
> *defend the orphan, plead for the widow.*

(Isaiah 1:13–17)

During this retreat we shall constantly be reminded of the prophetic words of the Pantocrator as he confronts us with his own burning vision of truth and righteousness. And we shall be faced with his glory which will shine into the dark places of our sinfulness, finitude and mortality. That is why the human being falls down in trembling awe, and a holy paralysis takes hold of the body and spirit in the presence of the divine energy.

In the seven letters the power of the Roman emperor is mighty but temporal, and the sovereignty of Christ is the sovereignty of Love.

DIVINE CHRIST AND HUMAN JESUS

We have already seen that the Orthodox icon of the Pantocrator is a true reflection of the Risen Christ presented in the Apocalypse at the end of the first century. We must also affirm that this is the same One who meets us in the gospels as the compassionate Physician and Saviour Jesus. No wedge should be placed between Jesus and the Christ. Unfortunately we have often domesticated him, projecting our own images of what we have wanted him to be, making such cultural accommodations so that he becomes manageable and does not interfere with the way in which we want to live our lives.

We should derive our image of Jesus from the New Testament documents instead of reading our own perspective into the Bible passages. If we did that we should be challenged as Peter was in the midst of his daily task of fishing on Galilee (Luke 5:8), and at the same time be aware of the searing love and mercy of the Apocalyptic Christ.

21

There never was a sweet, effeminate Jesus of some cloying Victorian prints, or imaged by sentimental theologians who had never been exposed to the horrors of world wars, holocaust and nuclear weaponry. There was, and is, a gentle Jesus, but his gentleness is the merciful aspect of his divinity shown to sinners who are cast down in their need, to fearful and frightened people who do not know where to turn, and to victims of sickness and violence throughout the world. And it goes without saying that he is powerfully gentle to little children who are close to his heart.

So as we approach Christ's message to the first of the seven churches, let us look more closely at the Christ of John's vision.

THE RISEN CHRIST IN GLORY

There is a trinitarian pattern of the mystery of God's salvation in the New Testament, and especially in the book of Revelation. In our present context we have John communicating the mystery of God the Father, being caught up in the Spirit, and describing, as far as human language allows, the wonder of the Christ whose silver-trumpeting voice sounded behind him.

> Write what you see and send it to the seven churches, to Ephesus, to Smyrna, to Pergamum, to Thyatira, to Sardis, to Philadelphia, and to Laodicea (1:11).

Here is a dramatic vision of Christ communicating his divine will to the Church through the prophetic word. This in no way denies the direct access which every believer has to the living

Lord, but it does give primacy to the objective revelation through the sure word of prophecy which is the guide and inspiration of all private revelation (2 Peter 1:19–21).

John is to commit the revelation to a written scroll, and the messenger is to take it from Patmos to the mainland harbour of Ephesus, making the rough clockwise journey to the seven churches. There it would be read on the first-day celebration of the eucharist, alongside the Old Testament and those portions of the gospel story and epistles as were available in Asia Minor.

As John turns to look, immediately light from the seven golden lampstands reveals the human but glorified Christ who is both Son of Man and Son of God, his long robe and golden girdle indicating his divine role as prophet, priest and king. Yet this is no mere angel, for the 'Ancient of Days' of the book of Daniel (7:9) shines through the description.

John is filled with awe and is smitten by the radiant holiness of the vision, yet all the details are perceived and interpreted, and the intricate thematic aspects of the Christ are worked into the opening words to each of the seven churches:

- **Ephesus**: The words of him who holds the seven stars in his right hand (2:1).
- **Smyrna**: The words of the first and the last, who was dead and came to life (2:8).
- **Pergamum**: The words of him who has the sharp two-edged sword (2:12).
- **Thyatira**: The words of the Son of God, who has eyes like a flame of fire, and whose feet are like burnished bronze (2:18).
- **Sardis**: The words of him who has the seven spirits of God and the seven stars (3:1).

23

- **Philadelphia**: The words of the holy one, the true one, who has the key of David, who opens and no one will shut, who shuts and no one opens (3:7).
- **Laodicea**: The words of the Amen, the faithful and true witness (3:14).

It is as if the primal vision given to John contains the whole of what will be communicated to the churches, and that one full and glorious vision of Christ is enough, so that nothing else is required.

But just as the wonderful vision of the Transfiguration filled the three disciples on Tabor with glory, while the other nine were squabbling on the plain below (Mark 9:14–29), so the message needs to be spelled out to the seven churches on earth and driven home in black and white.

The relationship of the primal vision to the lettered scroll is that of the person of the beloved to the love letter. But there are times when the beloved shines through the lines of the letter, and his perfume fills the senses of the lover. The purpose of the letters to the churches is encapsulated in the words of Mary Lathbury's hymn:

> Break now the Bread of Life
>   Dear Lord, to me,
> As once you broke the bread
>   Beside the sea;
> Beyond the sacred page
>   I seek You, Lord,
> My Spirit yearns for You,
>   O Living Word.

We shall take up the description of the Pantocrator as we meditate on the various letters, but immediately we are faced with the Ancient of Days whose hair, white as wool, speaks of his eternity and purity – the Alpha and Omega whose glory is shared by the Father and the Son (1:8; 22:13).

His eyes shine with penetrating love, the burnished bronze of his feet indicates steadfastness, swiftness and beauty, and his voice is resplendent with the beating of the waves around the coast of Patmos, echoing the eternal pulse of the Cosmic Lord.

The Risen Christ does not only stand among his churches on earth, but holds the heavenly *ecclesia* in his right hand as seven stars. This earthly-heavenly nature of the Church of God is a truth which the churches of Asia Minor need to learn as the roaring of the persecuting Antichrist sounds in their ears.

The power of the state seems all pervasive to the little churches dotted around the province, and the demand for Caesar-worship implies the penalty of suffering and death. In this situation, the vision of the Christ holding the seven stars in his right hand, with the two-edged sword of the Spirit issuing from his mouth, and the outshining radiance of his glory on his face, is enough to empower the feeble believers, and to put the enemies to flight.

This is the vision to hold before our eyes and hearts when the troubles of the world threaten us, when our sins and sicknesses are about to overwhelm us or when the powers of darkness engulf us in our weakness.

This is the Christ who still stands in and above the world, and who will one day return in glory to redeem all who are his own, initiating a new heaven and a new earth in his eternal kingdom of peace.

25

But for the present we fall before him in awe and adoration, and we hear his words as he lays his right hand upon us:

Do not be afraid; I am the first and the last, and the living one. I was dead, and see, I am alive for ever and ever; and I have the keys of Death and of Hades (1:17f.).

Goddess Artemis of Ephesus

Ephesus

Letter to the Church at Ephesus

Revelation 2:1–7

To the angel of the church in Ephesus write:

These are the words of him who holds the seven stars in his right hand, who walks among the seven golden lampstands:

I know your works, your toil and your patient endurance. I know that you cannot tolerate evildoers; you have tested those who claim to be apostles but are not, and have found them to be false. I also know that you are enduring patiently and bearing up for the sake of my name, and that you have not grown weary.

But I have this against you, that you have abandoned the love you had at first. Remember then from what you have fallen; repent, and do the works you did at first. If not, I will come to you and remove your lampstand from its place, unless you repent. Yet this is to your credit: you hate the works of the Nicolaitans, which I also hate.

Let anyone who has an ear listen to what the Spirit is saying to the churches. To everyone who conquers, I will give permission to eat from the tree of life that is in the paradise of God.

Spent Enthusiasm: The Church at Ephesus

Ephesus was the foremost city of Asia Minor, and its greatest harbour, and has been called *Lumen Asiae*, the Light of Asia. It was set at the mouth of the river Cayster, and three great roads converged on the city. The great trade route from the Euphrates wound through Colossae and Laodicea to Ephesus. The road from Galatia came into Ephesus via Sardis, bringing all the trade of the province. The third road came from the south, adding the trade of the Meander valley to that of the Cayster valley. It was through Ephesus that Christians were brought from Asia Minor to be fed to the lions in the Roman arena, and that is why the martyr Ignatius (d. 107) called it *the Highway of the Martyrs*.

Dean Farrer suggests that the fabulous list of merchandise described in Revelation 18:12f. is a picture of the markets of Ephesus. The big problem was keeping the harbour open, as it constantly tended to silt up, so that great labour and watchfulness were required.

Ephesus was also politically important. The Romans had granted it the status of a free city with self-government, which freed it from occupation by Roman troops. It had its own magistrates and a democratically elected governing body with an assembly (*ecclesia*) of all its citizens. You see this in operation when the town clerk tried to keep order in the uproar recorded in Acts 19:23–41.

Ephesus was also the centre of the Pan-Ionian Games in the month Artemesion (May), sacred to the goddess Artemis (Diana). These celebrations, together with the pageantry of the regular visit of the Roman governor, made Ephesus the centre of colourful Graeco-Roman glory. There were a number of famous temples in the city erected to the divinity of the Roman Emperors Claudius and Nero, and in later times it added temples to Hadrian and Severus.

But the greatest glory of Ephesus was the Temple of Artemis. In John's time it was the third such temple, one of the seven wonders of the world, 425 feet long, 220 feet wide and 60 feet high. The mysterious image of the goddess was so old, its origins were unknown, and many believed it had fallen from heaven. But it was no lovely Diana, the huntress goddess, chaste and fair, but a black, squat, grotesque figure, many-breasted as a symbol of fertility, holding a club and a trident with arcane and unknown inscriptions around its base, and sacred to millions of people.

Attached to the temple were many eunuch priests. Some said this was because Artemis was too fastidious to have a virile male near her, but others said it was because it was dangerous for a normal male to approach her as she was lascivious and sexually insatiable. There were also many hundreds of priestesses who were temple prostitutes. The worship was often full of shouts, wailing, wild music, accompanied by hysterical and emotional frenzy, leading to orgiastic rites and temple prostitution.

In an inner sanctum of the temple there was a completely safe area for depositing valuables and precious stones, which was not violated even in civil strife and an unstable world. The temple also possessed the right of asylum, a bowshot's length around the perimeter, and this area contained a large collection of criminals. But quite apart from the criminal groupings, the general reputation of the Ephesians was one of immorality, superstition and idolatory.

The story of Ephesus, great as it was, became one of eventual decline. Because of the silt which the Cayster river brought down, and the lack of attentive care, the harbour became a marshy growth of weeds, so that today the greatest harbour of Asia Minor is silted up, with the old city in ruins and about six miles from the sea!

Ephesus is especially significant for us because it was here that St Paul founded the Christian Church in AD 50–55, from which the whole province was evangelized, 'so that all the residents of Asia, both Jews and Greeks, heard the word of the Lord' (Acts 19:10). After AD 70 it became the chief centre of the Christian faith in the East.

Timothy was its first bishop (1 Timothy 1:3), and saintly and charismatic believers such as Aquila, Priscilla and Apollos ministered there (Acts 18:24ff.). Paul's farewell address to the Ephesian elders is moving and beautiful (Acts 20:17–36), revealing more of the tenderness, warmth and vulnerability of the apostle than some would have imagined:

When [Paul] had finished speaking, he knelt down with them all and prayed. There was much weeping among them all; they embraced Paul and kissed him, grieving especially because of what he had said, that they would not see him again. Then they brought him to the ship.

We have a lovely picture of St John the disciple bringing Mary the Mother of Jesus to Ephesus at the end of her life, where she fell asleep and died. As Archbishop R.C. Trench wrote: 'Nowhere did the word of God find a kindlier soil, strike root more deeply or bear fairer fruits of faith and love.'

Day 1 Morning
Orthodox and Energetic

There is something strange here. From the letter it appears that there is both orthodoxy and a busy activism operating in the Ephesian church — yet they are accused of abandoning their first love for Christ.

The first words of the letter direct attention to the Christ who holds the seven stars in his right hand, and walks among the seven golden lampstands. In other words, Christ is the Pantocrator holding the churches together in unity in the right hand of his power, so that no one and nothing can snatch them from his grasp (John 10:28).

Both stars and lampstands symbolize the churches, and Christ's presence among them and holding them manifests their unity. Denominations, schisms and heresies divide, but there is only one Church, one mystical Body of Christ, and he is the Head.

In these days it is precious to me to be an ecumenical Christian, learning from and ministering to other communions in the Body of Christ. In my previous parish and Franciscan ministry I was always in touch with other Christians who longed to know more of the fullness of Christ's love, and it is even more true now that I am exploring the hermit life. I am aware of the theological symbolism of Christ walking among the lampstands of his Church on earth, and holding the unified Church in his right hand in heaven.

The unity is in the Holy Spirit, the diversity is manifest among Anglicans, Baptists, Catholics, Methodists, Orthodox,

Pentecostals, from the house church movement, and others. At best they are like stars radiant with the light of Christ, or lampstands of witness fed by the oil of the Holy Spirit. Christ holds them, Christ walks among them, and in the coming again of Christ their unity will be fully achieved and known.

The Risen Christ commends the Ephesian believers for their toil, patience and endurance, for unflagging energy and abundant activity, especially in sniffing out false doctrine, trying the claims of wandering, itinerant preachers who falsely claimed to be prophets and apostles. We recall the warning of the apostle Paul to the Ephesian elders some decades previously:

> I know that after I have gone, savage wolves will come in among you, not sparing the flock. Some even from your own group will come distorting the truth in order to entice the disciples to follow them (Acts 20:29f.).

These are days of exclusivist sects, many of them claiming a hot line to God, imposing a puritanical rigidity of doctrine on their followers and passing judgement on everyone outside their particular fold. Among the mainline churches there is a hairsbreadth of difference between maintaining soundness of doctrine and espousing a bigoted dogmatism. The joy and sorrow of being an ecumenical Christian lie in holding to the centre of the faith, which is Christ, and cherishing the particular truths which your own communion holds tenaciously, while at the same time appreciating and understanding the truths, insights and liturgical practices of other Christians in other parts of the Church.

The Ephesian Christians had expended much energy,

endured much suffering, examined false teachers and hypocrites, and had taken to heart the discourse of Paul to the Ephesian elders which had already been committed to writing:

I did not shrink from declaring to you the whole purpose of God. Keep watch over yourselves and over all the flock, of which the Holy Spirit has made you overseers, to shepherd the church of God that he obtained with the blood of his own Son (Acts 20:27f.).

But in the process of such examination, purification, weeding out false teachers and standing in judgement over faith and morals, something sad seems to have happened: 'I have this against you, that you have abandoned the love you had at first' (2:4). Did Christ mean the love which burned in zeal towards God, the pattern of which was his own incarnation and redemption? Or did he mean the fervent love which the Ephesian believers had for one another?

The trouble about heresy-hunting is that theological discernment is easily replaced by a judgemental attitude, which in turn leads to bigotry and fanaticism, and itself falls into a far worse heresy – that of hatred. And the strange and awful truth is that this describes the mindset of some religious people – though it is far from the spirit of Christ. Jesus warns against such pseudo-religion:

They will put you out of the synagogues. Indeed, an hour is coming when those who kill you will think that by doing so they are offering worship to God (John 16:2).

This scenario is spelled out in Umberto Eco's *The Name of the Rose*, and the film of that book turns inquisition into the bloody and terrible thing that it is – an instrument of Satan under the cloak of religion.

This is the fundamentalist attitude which can logically and biblically burn witches, stone adulterers, justify apartheid and slaughter whole communities or nations for the sake of *our* interpretation, to protect the purity of *our* faith, or to preserve *our* religious heritage.

If love for God leads to such inhuman and bigoted attitudes, then we have to question if it is indeed the love of God, and whether we have misread the story. Love of God and of fellow creatures run together. The first great commandment is to love God with heart, mind, soul and strength – utterly, rapturously, unreservedly! But immediately following on such divine outpouring is the overflow towards neighbour, friend and enemy.

And who is neighbour? Well, Samaritan or Jew, Catholic or Quaker, Buddhist or Sikh; and we are increasingly realizing that the voices of oppressed and violated animals, and the ecological balance of the world are included, and are our responsibility. Thomas Merton speaks of a startling implication of the Incarnation of God in Christ when he says:

> *In becoming man, God became not only Jesus Christ, but also potentially every man and woman that ever existed. In Christ, God became not only 'this' man, but also, in a broader and more mystical sense, yet no less truly, 'every man'.*
>
> (*New Seeds of Contemplation*, pp. 294f.)

It is a matter of becoming loving and open to all people, and this extends to all sentient creatures, and ultimately to the whole of creation. It is a life-long task, but is the way of Jesus, in contrast to the heresy-hunting and dogmatic mentality which may have overtaken the Ephesian church.

I am not suggesting that we sink our profoundly held beliefs in an indifferent tolerance that holds nothing distinctively precious and basic. Such a religion, apart from not being worth anything, would certainly not produce martyrs! What we must do is to tune our hearts and minds to the risen Christ, the centre of our faith. We must hold the essential truths of our revealed faith precious – for it is a faith to die for – and to live for. But above all, we must remember that this is not a religion of dogmatic propositions, but the revelation of God's love in Christ.

I do not water down the amazing revelation of the divinity of Christ when I dialogue with a Buddhist friend. I do not belittle Christ's deity to fit the measure of a human prophet, charismatic guru or healer. I commend Christ the Saviour in all his fullness – but I also listen to my Buddhist friend and appreciate the words of wisdom he has to share with me. The outcome is that he enters into an understanding of Christ's compassion, and I discover the hidden Christ in so much of what he has to share. This is not compromise but dialogue, and even if we disagree it is in the spirit of seeking for truth.

Perhaps the Ephesians lost their first love because of bigoted heresy-hunting which caused them to lose sight of the crucified Jesus. He gives them a threefold counsel: Remember! Repent! Rededicate! But these words we shall turn to this evening.

*

Prayer

Lord Jesus, Lover of Souls:

*You stand in the midst of the churches and call us to fullness of faith
and charity of life;*

*Grant that we may earnestly, fervently and faithfully interpret your
    word and explore our faith, but let us not confuse dogma with living
    truth, nor in affirming doctrine fail to be enfolded in your compas-
    sion.*

*You call us to remembrance of past sins, to repentance for present atti-
    tudes, and to renewed dedication;*

*Grant us a listening heart to hear what the Spirit is saying to the
    churches.   Amen.*

*

Response

Make a list of the doctrines or teachings that you hold precious.
Ask yourself whether they make you a better human being. Is
there an increase in love, in openness of heart and common
charity?

If not, ask yourself whether you have the doctrines right or
whether your religion is less than your humanity.

The Risen Christ confronted the religious and persecuting
Saul on the Damascus road and melted his bigoted heart. What
about yours?

*

Day 1 Evening
Losing Your First Love

If this morning we listened to Christ's word to his Church, this evening's word becomes intensely personal – from Christ to the believer. These are not separate issues, but there is a distinction to be made, for it is easy to lose the specific cutting edge of a personal conscience when compromises are made for the common good.

It is possible for a herd mentality to develop, and for the corporate body to become involved in relationships and decisions which the individual would shrink from. I always tune in to my personal conscience when 'defence of our religious (or national) heritage' is called for, or even when many thousands of pounds are channelled into the erection or repair of church organs and religious buildings. It is well for us to remember that the seven churches of Asia Minor knew simplicity and poverty (with the exception of Laodicea) while munificent pagan temples prospered and a pseudo-religious state persecuted them.

It is not insignificant that in this ancient city, dependent upon its harbour for trade and travel, people ultimately allowed the river Cayster to silt up the harbour due to neglect. St Paul's warning counsel to the elders (Acts 20:17–36), and the influence of Timothy, the first bishop, was sufficient to cause Christ to commend the Ephesian church for its early toil, endurance and discernment. But as time went by the spiritual harbour silted up too, and energy was expended on the externals of religion, so that the later counsel was to repentance and warning: 'I have this against you, that you have abandoned the love you had at first' (2:4).

The language is that of relationship, of affectivity, the heart of faith, which is love for Jesus Christ, the Saviour. The New Testament is full of fervent love and zeal for Christ, spilling over in the Acts of the Apostles, and enjoined and encouraged in the epistles:

> *Let love be genuine; hate what is evil, hold fast to what is good; love one another with mutual affection; outdo one another in showing honour. Do not lag in zeal, be ardent in spirit, serve the Lord (Romans 12:9ff.).*

If we wonder what kind of fervent first love marked the early Ephesian church, which they had now abandoned, we should look back into Paul's Ephesian epistle which was filled with an amazing trinitarian expectation for this very church:

> *I bow my knees before the Father, from whom every family in heaven and on earth takes its name. I pray that, according to the riches of his glory, he may grant that you may be strengthened in your inner being with power through his Spirit, and that Christ may dwell in your hearts through faith, as you are being rooted and grounded in love. I pray that you may have the power to comprehend, with all the saints, what is the breadth and length and height and depth, and to know the love of Christ that surpasses knowledge, so that you may be filled with all the fullness of God (Ephesians 3:14ff.).*

This presents a frightening contrast with Christ's words to the same church in Revelation 2:1–7. Yet all is not lost – praise and blame are intermingled, and the silt may yet be cleared from the harbour. As you read these words, look into your own life. It is clear that you are not as bad as you might be, or as good as you could be. There are shades of grey, compromises and compassion mingling in a mixed life that has lost its early potential, and is lacking in vital direction.

We noted in this morning's meditation that the actual matter of religious dogmatism and speculation may have been the reason for the loss of true, affective devotion to Christ. Such preoccupations begin in subtle ways. I wonder what was going on when Paul wrote to Timothy, on his way to Macedonia:

> I urge you ... to remain in Ephesus so that you may instruct certain people not to teach any different doctrine, and not to occupy themselves with myths and endless genealogies that promote speculations rather than divine training that is known by faith. But the aim of such instruction is love that comes from a pure heart, a good conscience and sincere faith. Some people have deviated from these and turned to meaningless talk ... (1 Timothy 1:3ff.).

One of the strangest and saddest experiences is to meet a man or woman who seeks to hate what Christ hates without loving what Christ loves. The people referred to above were evidently argumentative people, and although the material of their argumentation was religious, the manner of their debate was destructive, manipulative and self-assertive. It is possible to win your argument and lose your humanity. This is what Paul means when he says that such people deviate from the way of Christ in their speculative and dogmatic arguing. The result is a loss of that first, genuine, heartfelt love for Christ which is the only real basis of spiritual religion.

Look at the threefold aim that Paul commends to Timothy — a pure heart, a good conscience and sincere faith. These are virtues which are communal as well as personal, but they must first be planted in the individual response to the love of Christ, for then they will overflow not only to fellow Christians but to all with whom we come into contact.

The only way by which the Ephesian Christians can win the pagans is by loving them into the kingdom of Christ. If their necessary debates are infused with compassion and joy instead of deteriorating into speculative strife, then people will be drawn into divine Love by the power of the Holy Spirit.

The three words with which we concluded our morning meditation indicate the path from a compromising loss of vitality to the restoration of that first love which burned so brightly. They are imperatives: Remember! Repent! Rededicate! The first word points to a recalling of the way things used to be. William Cowper encapsulates much of this in his sad but beautiful hymn 'O for a closer walk with God':

Where is the blessedness I knew
    When first I saw the Lord?
Where is the soul-refreshing view
    Of Jesus and his word?

What peaceful hours I once enjoyed!
    How sweet their memory still!
But they have left an aching void
    The world can never fill.

Such a remembrance is suffused with the spirit of true repentance, and just as the lover will weep tears of remembrance and longing over an estrangement from the beloved, so such tears will heal the wound, draw lover and beloved together again. If the cost is turning from other idols and relationships which have caused the rupture, then that is gladly done, so that love may flow again.

Love is the only way to heal a betrayal of love, and this is the way of Christ. Yet this is not incompatible with Christ's dire warning of the neglect of love: 'I will come to you and remove your lampstand from its place, unless you repent,' he says, for his love is a fiery and searing passion that brooks no compromise. This is the godly jealousy (2 Corinthians 11:2) which cannot coexist with other lovers. Such compromise only adulterates the passion of a pure heart, leading to dissipation of vital energies and the loss of 'first love'.

The removal of the lampstand relates to the loss of witness, the withdrawal of the oil of the Holy Spirit, and the extinguishing of the radiant light of guidance and clarity in our dark world. It applies to the individual believer, to the local church and to the Church catholic. Israel was called to be 'a light to the nations' and the Church 'the light of the world' (Isaiah 42:6; Matthew 5:14), to reflect the universal love of God, and failure to do so brings its own judgement.

If the individual or the church/Church loses the first love of dedication to God and compassion for a needy world, and perpetuates a different Gospel which has to do with manipulative power, money or territory, then the lampstand is removed, the witness decays and love is extinguished. The judgement of God is the loss of love, and this is ultimately what hell is —

the lapsing into the non-being of darkness and eternal loss.

Yet the last word is not one of judgement, but of growth, fertility and fruitfulness: 'To those who win the victory I will give the right to eat of the tree of life that grows in the Garden of God' (2:7; GNB). With this final word so many beautiful images come to mind – from the paradise of God in Genesis 2:8–14, to its restoration in the final chapters of the Apocalypse (22:1f.). Added to this is the lovely picture of the River of God in Ezekiel 47:1–12, which itself is a transcendent prophecy of ultimate healing and restoration.

This is the kind of abundant healing and fruitfulness in store for the Ephesian Christians who respond with a listening heart to what the Spirit is saying. The final outcome is the vision of paradise in the last chapter of the Apocalypse:

> *On either side of the river, is the tree of life with its twelve kinds of fruit, producing its fruit each month; and the leaves of the tree are for the healing of the nations (22:2).*

*

Prayer

Lord Jesus Christ, restorer of paradise:

You have shone into my heart with the radiance of divine love, and given me a place among your faithful people;

If my heart loses its purity, if my conscience is stained and if my faith becomes insincere, then let me be judged by the discipline of your chastisement.

Restore to me that first love which was kindled by your Holy Spirit, and let it shine in the dark places of your world.   Amen.

*

Response

Bearing in mind the will of Christ for (a) the believer; (b) the local church and (c) the Church catholic, do you feel that in these three categories there has been a loss of first love and a misrepresentation of the love of God to the world?

In which ways would you think this is true doctrinally and practically? Can you see what steps may be taken to heal and redeem this situation?

For yourself, take up and read the whole of William Cowper's hymn 'O for a closer walk with God', and make your confession and rededicate your life to God's love.

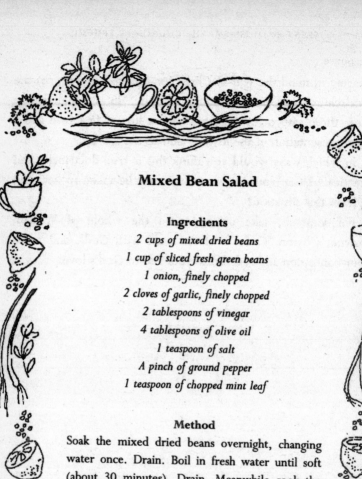

Mixed Bean Salad

Ingredients

2 cups of mixed dried beans
1 cup of sliced fresh green beans
1 onion, finely chopped
2 cloves of garlic, finely chopped
2 tablespoons of vinegar
4 tablespoons of olive oil
1 teaspoon of salt
A pinch of ground pepper
1 teaspoon of chopped mint leaf

Method

Soak the mixed dried beans overnight, changing water once. Drain. Boil in fresh water until soft (about 30 minutes). Drain. Meanwhile cook the fresh beans in a little boiling water until tender (about 10 minutes). Drain, but keep this water for stock. Put all the beans in a serving bowl and mix with the onion, garlic, vinegar and oil. Sprinkle on the salt, pepper and mint leaf. Mix again.

Yoghurt may be substituted for the vinegar and oil dressing. Serve with fresh tomatoes and wedges of lemon.

46

Domitian the Persecutor

The Crown of Life

Smyrna

Letter to the Church at Smyrna
Revelation 2:8–11

And to the angel of the church in Smyrna write:

These are the words of the first and the last, who was dead and came to life:

I know your affliction and your poverty, even though you are rich. I know the slander on the part of those who say that they are Jews and are not, but are a synagogue of Satan.

Do not fear what you are about to suffer. Beware, the devil is about to throw some of you into prison so that you may be tested, and for ten days you will have affliction. Be faithful unto death, and I will give you the crown of life.

Let anyone who has an ear listen to what the Spirit is saying to the churches. Whoever conquers will not be harmed by the second death.

Persecution and Glory: The Church at Smyrna

We come to the second in the necklace of the seven churches. Smyrna was destroyed in the sixth century BC, but refounded in the fourth century BC, ranking as the most beautiful of cities in Asia Minor, though Lysimachus' architect omitted the drains! It has continued to the present day, a centre of learning for the Eastern Orthodox Church.

It lies about thirty-five miles north of Ephesus in a natural gulf, in an enclosed harbour, at the end of one of the great trade roads of the Hermus valley, with its harbour trade outlet, especially in wines.

Smyrna was always a favourite of Rome, and back in 196 BC a temple to *Dea Roma*, Goddess Rome, was erected. In competing with eleven other cities to erect a temple to the emperor Tiberius, as a god, the senate awarded the honour to Smyrna in AD 26. This temple may well still have been standing in John's time.

As Artemis was the great goddess in Ephesus, so Dionysius was extremely popular in Smyrna, though there were also temples to Cybele, Apollo, Asclepius, Aphrodite and Zeus – gods and lords many (1 Corinthians 8:5). Dionysius represented the mysterious productive and intoxicating powers of nature, dispensing joy and fertility, and dispersing sorrow and grief. Dionysius' myth of death and resurrection was enacted in Smyrna, and the priests who presided were presented with crowns. All this gives point to the One who truly was dead and came to life, and who offers to the faithful the crown of life.

The city possessed a famous stadium, a library and a large public theatre, with an important monument to Homer, whose birthplace it claimed to be, just as it claimed to be first in Caesar worship. It certainly was a centre for the worship of the emperor, and it was in Domitian's time that the saying 'Caesar is Lord' was taken absolutely seriously.

Under the *Pax Romana*, the Roman peace, travel could take place with less fear, trade could be conducted and letters sent in security. Pirates and brigands became fewer and were condemned, and strict and impartial Roman justice was available. In this atmosphere people were willing to offer gratitude, and then worship to the spirit of Rome, which evolved into *Dea Roma*, the Goddess Rome.

The early emperors disdained this evolving worship, but then it became tolerated, acceptable, official and compulsory in periodic stages in different geographical locations. The emperor became a god, and this was the very thing that provided political unification for the vast empire of races and nations of the known world. The spirit of Rome was universal, the *Pax Romana* was beneficent, the Roman justice was appreciated – and so worship was gradually given.

At the time of the letters to the seven churches of Asia Minor in the reign of Domitian, emperor worship was in place, and all citizens were under compulsion to burn a pinch of incense on the altar to the divinity of Caesar, and were given a certificate to guarantee that they had been witnessed to have done so. But this the Christian could not do!

The Christian could not worship the emperor because Christ was the judge of both emperor and empire. And that the state could not accept. Here were little David and great Goliath as the tiny early Church stood against the universal empire. Not everyone did stand the test, but those who endured by the witness of martyrdom became the triumphant spiritual soldiers of Christ, for the first Christians would not enlist in earthly armies.

This was why the Apocalypse was written. Its symbolism was clear to the Christian but totally puzzling to hostile Roman authorities. The book said that Rome and its empire were temporal but Christ was eternal. The martyr was triumphant in the very moment of defeat, and all the power and authority of a pagan state were accounted as nothing before the Pantocrator, the Lord of heaven and earth. The Roman Tacitus, who was certainly no Christian, wrote in his *Annals* (xv. 44):

> *Mockery of every sort was added to their deaths. Covered with the skins of beasts, they were torn by dogs and perished, or were nailed to the crosses, or were doomed to the flames and burnt, to serve as a nightly illumination when daylight had expired. Nero offered his gardens for the spectacle, and was exhibiting a show in the circus, while he mingled with the people in the dress of a charioteer or stood aloft in a car.*

And Ignatius, who passed through Asia Minor, on his way to a Roman martyrdom in AD 107, wrote in his letter to the Ephesians:

51

Come fire, and cross, and grapplings with wild beasts, cuttings and manglings, wrenchings of bones, breaking of limbs, crushing of my whole body, come cruel tortures of the devil to assail me. Only be it mine to attain unto Jesus Christ.

Such courage and fearlessness in the face of persecution and martyrdom was a mark of the infant churches in the days of the Apocalypse. Caesar's claim to divinity was blasphemy to the Christians, and they would have nothing to do with a totalitarian state which demanded complete allegiance of body and soul – this was the spirit of antichrist. E.A. Edghill, in *The Spirit of Power*, puts it this way:

Caesar worship had been growing apace in the provinces, and it was there apparently that the first shock of conflict was felt. Domitian had gone further than his predecessors in asserting his own divinity. Official proclamations insisted on the recognition of the Emperor as dominus ac deus noster. *Nowhere did this imperial cultus find more immediate and lasting favour than in Asia. Here the loyalty and gratitude of the provincials caused it to assume the character of a popular and patriotic religion. On high days of public festival, imposing ceremonies in connection with the imperial cult preceded the festivities. The slightest reluctance to identify oneself with the joy and games, the sacrifices or spectacles then celebrated, was sufficient to expose a man to the charge of calculated and deliberate disloyalty. The offence to local feeling would be deep, the affront to the majesty of Caesar incapable of being passed over. The Epistle of Peter, and, still more, the Apocalypse of John, illustrate this state of things.*

It is to such a situation that Christ speaks words of unqualified praise to the believers in Smyrna, beginning: 'These are the words of the first and the last, who was dead and came to life' (2:8).

Day 2 Morning
Christ Who was Dead and is Alive

Christ is the first and the last. These first words to the church in Smyrna (2:8) pick up the same words in the earlier vision (1:17). It is an affirmation that right in the midst of a pagan city, where persecution was a gathering storm upon the near horizon, where imprisonment, torture and death threatened at any moment – *there*, in the midst of the church, is Christ.

He is the *First* – the One before whom nothing had come into being; he is the *Last* – the One in whom all things earthly and heavenly are to be brought to consummation (Ephesians 1:10).

But this is not simply an affirmation of some faraway deity who runs the whole cosmic show, but who has no intimate concern for his creatures. His creatures are his sons and daughters, his loved ones, and that is why he fulfils his gospel promise: 'Where two or three are gathered in my name, I am there among them' (Matthew 18:20).

Between that gospel promise and the crisis in Smyrna he had undergone such darkness and suffering, exhausting the abyss of death and hell on their behalf, for

none of the ransomed ever knew
how deep were the waters crossed,
or how dark was the night that the Lord passed through
ere he found his sheep that was lost.

The Christ who took upon himself such a passion, and claimed such a victory, reminds the believers in Smyrna that there is no depth of suffering but that he has not been there, and no height of glory but that he will not carry them there with him.

This is what his next word means – 'I know!' It is not simply that he knows things *about* us, but that he *knows us* through and through. It is a knowledge which carries with it understanding, recognition and compassion. The old negro spiritual goes:

Nobody knows the troubles I've seen,
Nobody knows but Jesus.

And because he knows, that is sufficient. The awareness that God knows, and therefore cares, is one which has fortified believers through the ages. There are whole passages of scripture which overflow with relief and joy, breaking out into singing:

O Lord, you have searched me and known me.
You know when I sit down and when I rise up;
* you discern my thoughts from far away ...*
Such knowledge is too wonderful for me;
* it is so high that I cannot attain it.*
*   (Psalm 139:1,6)*

To each of the seven churches this word of knowledge is given, imparting immense comfort to the struggling and faithful Christians in Smyrna, but awakening the indifferent and arrogant members of the Laodicean church to a realization of the scrutiny of the all-seeing One (3:15).

We may not be threatened with religious or political persecution (though for some European readers this may be exactly what is happening), but Christ knows just what our situation is. 'I know your *affliction*,' says Jesus – this is the word *thlipsis* which means *pressure*. It can refer to the heavy weight by which the oil is crushed out in the olive press, or to the agony of a man who is crushed by a great boulder laid upon him.

What is your affliction as you read? Is it the pressure of domestic circumstances which you cannot share with others? The breakdown of a loving relationship? The heavy weight of facing terminal illness in your own or a loved one's life?

For the Smyrnaean believer it could mean being arrested at any moment, flung into a foetid prison cell, taken out to be tortured or to face death by burning or by being torn apart by beasts. There are many ways used by false religion and secular states to crush and oppress ordinary people, but right in the midst of it all the risen Lord says: 'I *know*! I have been there. I am there with you at this moment. I will carry you through.' The simple refrain has it:

Standing somewhere in the shadows you'll find Jesus,
He's the only One who cares and understands;
Standing somewhere in the shadows you will find him,
And you'll know him by the nail-prints in his hands.

Christ also speaks a pertinent word about poverty. In Britain we are making millionaires by the dubious method of a national lottery, while at the same time widening the gulf between the top and bottom in the social scale. We shall refer to this again, but contrast now the attitude of the poor people of Smyrna and the rich ones of Laodicea. Jesus says to the first: 'I know you are poor, but you are truly rich.' But to the Laodiceans he says:

'You say you are rich, but you are wretched, pitiable, poor, blind and naked' (3:17).

Poverty is a strange word, for if it is a voluntary surrender of what is superfluous it becomes a joyful simplicity – and that is what the Franciscan vow of poverty is about. But if it is destitution, penury and deprivation then it can be soul-destroying. There should be a radical difference between the followers of Christ and people of the world in this respect. Those who claim the name of Christ should live in voluntary poverty, 'living simply that others may simply live'. But perhaps it is obvious that we are more like the church in Laodicea than that in Smyrna. And our rewards will be appropriate!

Christ is speaking to a situation in Smyrna where believers' homes could be pillaged, their jobs lost, their lives forfeit – poverty indeed. But in the face of all this Christ calls them to be faithful in life and death because that is not the end of the story.

Looking at the text again you will see that there is also religious persecution from the Jews. There was a substantial population of Jews in Smyrna, as in the other cities, and they were among the richest people, with much influence. The sad thing is that they turned upon the local Christians, not only reporting them to the secular authorities, but (as we shall see this evening), themselves carrying fuel for the martyr's flame.

This is a delicate point in our meditation, for wherever there is even a suggestion of anti-semitism we must look deep into our own attitudes, and examine the bloody history of crusade, pogrom and holocaust in the history of the Church. The sad fact is that the three great monotheistic faiths have been guilty of bloody persecution and massacre, and as I never tire of saying – no religion is better than bad religion. It causes me immense pain whenever religious people resort to arms in so-called defence of their faith or heritage, but especially when they persecute one another, and do so in the name of the Prince of Peace. I would abjure a religion which demanded violence and killing. By the grace and mercy of God many undeserving sinners will be among the saved, but there is only a remnant who truly reflect the compassion of Christ. It is time for self-examination.

We shall consider the rest of Christ's words to Smyrna being told out this evening, in the story of its greatest martyr-bishop, but there is one thing more to be said before we conclude this meditation. It is a clear reference to the source of evil that gives rise to hatred, cruelty, persecution and martyrdom, and is found in the warning of verse 10: 'Beware, the devil is about to throw some of you into prison ...'

The New Testament is very clear that there are powers of light and of darkness behind the forces which are manifested in our world. It is not dualistic, for there is no doubt about the outcome – for the divine Love will overcome all obstacles at the last. But while history runs its course the conflict rages, and behind peoples and nations there are ranged dark powers of evil – just as the apostle had written to the Ephesian church:

> Put on the whole armour of God, so that you may be able to stand against the wiles of the devil. For our struggle is not against enemies of blood and flesh, but against the rulers, against the authorities, against the cosmic powers of this present darkness, against the spiritual forces of evil in the heavenly places (6:11f.).

There are dangers in an over-literal interpretation of scripture, especially in the Apocalypse, which abounds in angels and demons, and which can result in the present charismatic fascination with occult powers in a fundamentalist mode. This not only gives rise to the writing of fantastic novels of over five hundred pages, where the 'Captain of the Angelic Host' zooms around zapping all and sundry, but can result in the evasion of our own responsibility by laying the causes of all sin and sickness at the devil's door.

The New Testament writers do not do this. They acknowledge the reality of the angelic and demonic dimensions, but make human responsibility a primary response to God's demand for righteousness and justice.

There is such a thing as dark, cosmic conflict; there are dark powers behind warring nations, and such powers are not simply psychic, but have a more objective reality and influence. But our response to such a dimension of reality is that we should be concerned with the sovereignty of God, allying ourselves with loving compassion and prayerful watchfulness. The battle for good against evil will not be won by taking up carnal weapons or engaging in national or religious conflicts, but by the continual yielding of ourselves, as individuals and churches, to the non-violent witness of reconciliation and peace-making wherever there is a battlefield and wherever human rights are betrayed at any level.

This may involve us in national and international agencies of aid like Christian Aid, Tear Fund and CAFOD, or in non-violent confrontation with authorities through Amnesty International or the Campaign Against the Arms Trade or opposition to nuclear arms, or it may carry us physically into areas of conflict in direct peace-making. But all such prayerful action will be energized and fortified by the powers of light under the guidance of the Holy Spirit. By such prayer and action the powers of darkness will be put to flight. Christ's assurance to the believers in Smyrna were in anticipation of the final chapter of Revelation:

> See, I am coming soon; my reward is with me, to repay according to everyone's work. I am the Alpha and the Omega, the first and the last, the beginning and the end (22:12).

*

Prayer

Saviour Christ, risen from the dead:

Grant that in all our afflictions and conflicts on earth we may prove the strength of your Holy Spirit in standing against the powers of darkness;

Give us courage, in life or in death, to bear witness to the Prince of Peace, always motivated by divine compassion.   Amen.

*

Response

In remembering the churches of Asia Minor, find out more about the Greek and Russian Orthodox Churches, and especially the conflicts and trials of the Bosnian and Serbian Orthodox Churches.

Can you *do* anything to help? If so, do it!

*

Day 2 Evening
The Crown of Life

There is much talk of crowns in scripture, both crowns of royalty (*diadèma*) and crowns of victory (*stephanos*). It is the second with which we are concerned in our scripture passage, and it is worth giving some references to bring together the associations linked with them:

- Crown of Life (James 1:12)
- Crown of Righteousness (2 Timothy 4:8)
- Crown of Rejoicing (1 Thessalonians 2:19)
- Crown of Glory (1 Peter 5:4)
- Crown Incorruptible (1 Corinthians 9:25)

All these are of laurel leaves or flowers, and symbolize joy, victory, celebration and thanksgiving. They are awarded to athletes, victors and faithful servants at games, banquets and worship. A beautiful practice is the exchanging of crowns between bride and groom at an Orthodox wedding. Yet in all this we must not forget the reference Matthew 27:29 which transforms sorrow into joy:

> *The head that once was crowned with thorns*
> *Is crowned with glory now;*
> *A royal diadem adorns*
> *The mighty Victor's brow.*

But recall that it was not *diadèma* but *stephanos*!

Christ's promise to the martyr was a crown of life (2:10), and when this year I sent a card to Stephen, one of our Franciscan tertiaries, I reminded him that, like the protomartyr Stephen, his name meant 'a crown', and I quoted the hymn for St Stephen's Day:

> Glitters now the crown above you,
>   Figured in your sacred name:
> O that we who truly love you
>   May have portion in the same;
> In the dreadful day of judgement
>   Fearing neither sin nor shame.

The Book of Revelation is the only apocalypse in the canon of the New Testament, but there are other 'Christian' apocalypses, and one of them, 2 Esdras, is found among the books of the apocrypha. I mention this because there is included a beautiful passage about martyrs, crowns and glory which has a lovely surprise element in it, and which is sometimes read on All Saints Day:

> I, Ezra, saw on Mount Zion a great multitude that I could not number, and they all were praising the Lord with songs. In their midst was a young man of great stature, taller than any of the others, and on the head of each of them he placed a crown, but he was more exalted than they. And I was held spellbound. Then I asked an angel, 'Who are these, my lord?' He answered and said to me, 'These are they who have put off mortal clothing and have put on the immortal, and have confessed the name of God. Now they are being crowned and receive palms.' Then I said to

the angel, 'Who is that young man who is placing crowns on
them and putting palms in their hands?' He answered and said
to me, 'He is the Son of God, whom they confessed in the world.'
So I began to praise those who had stood valiantly for the name
of the Lord (2 Esdras 2:42—47).

The crown of thorns was exchanged for a crown of glory. The
faithful suffering of the martyrs of Smyrna was to be trans-
formed by the King of Martyrs, Jesus himself, who promised:
'Be faithful until death, and I will give you the crown of life'
(2:10).

In his *Ecclesiastical History* Eusebius tells the story of the
greatest martyr of Smyrna. It happened on the occasion of the
Stadium games in AD 155. Polycarp was bishop of Smyrna, and
like the warning in our text, he had been shown his martyrdom
in a dream in which his pillow caught fire.

The crowd had been stirred up with the excitement of a herd
mentality thirsting for blood, and the cry went up: 'Let Polycarp
be searched for.' A tortured slave revealed his whereabouts, and
when the police chief and his men found him they were offered
hospitality while Polycarp was given one hour for prayer.

Polycarp was an old man, a good man, a wise man, and on
the way, the chief tried to persuade him to burn a pinch of
incense, and say: 'Caesar is Lord', but Polycarp could only
confess with the Church that 'Jesus is Lord'.

The dramatic moment came when Polycarp entered the
arena full of faith, despite his age and the mood of the crowd.
The proconsul commanded him to revile Christ and make
sacrifice to Caesar or else to die.

Polycarp stood and confronted the proconsul, the crowd and

the powers of darkness, and said: 'Eighty-and-six years have I served him, and he has done me no wrong. How can I blaspheme my King who saved me?'

The proconsul threatened him with fire, and he replied: 'You threaten me with the fire that burns for a time and is quickly quenched, for you do not know the fire which awaits the wicked in the judgement to come ... Why are you waiting? Come, do what you will.'

Upon such words the crowd broke loose and brought fuel and kindling for the fire, the Jews even breaking their sabbath to participate in putting Polycarp to the flames.

The sad story is shot through with glory as Polycarp, unbound at the stake, breaks out in prayer, is enveloped by flames, and is pierced to death by the executioner, so that the crowd was amazed at the difference between the dying of the Christians and that of unbelievers. The element of judgement in the reproof given by Polycarp reflects the words spoken by Christ in our text. For those who indulge in violence and cruelty, in persecution, torture and killing the people of God, there is on the horizon, beyond the warning of persecution, the shadow of the second death (2:11).

The promise is that for those who live in faithfulness, who die in martyrdom, there is deliverance from the second death which is the death of the spirit. The question arises – who is condemned to this second death, and in what does it consist?

Again, there are many dramatic symbols and metaphors in the Apocalypse, not to be taken *literally* but to be taken *seriously*. Those who do not take judgement seriously are not able to understand the seriousness and wonder of the love of Christ, who for us sinners underwent and exhausted the darkness of judgement. Again, it is the crown language which expresses it, and this time in the context of Bach's Passion Chorale:

> O Sacred Head once wounded,
>   With grief and pain weighed down,
> How scornfully surrounded
>   With thorns, thine only crown!
> How pale art thou with anguish,
>   With sore abuse and scorn!
> How does that visage languish
>   Which once was bright as morn.
>
> O Lord of life and glory,
>   What bliss till now was thine!
> I read the wondrous story,
>   I joy to call thee mine.
> Thy grief and thy compassion
>   Were all for sinners' gain;
> Mine, mine was the transgression,
>   But thine the deadly pain.

The judgement symbolism and metaphor of the Apocalypse speak of the death of the soul — alienation, estrangement and ultimate separation from the light, love and life of God. Therefore the second death is a dimming of the light, a losing of the love and a lapsing from the life which is the fullness of God's being. This is a self-judgement, for the divine mercy is open to all, and the cry of the heavenly Father for his lost children sounds the depths of eternity.

The man or woman who can ultimately reject the divine

Love, after understanding what it means to refuse the offer of life, condemn themselves to the second death. We do not know the effect of such a decision upon such people, save that ultimately they lapse into non-being and annihilation, for rebellion and wickedness cannot coexist eternally with the eternal Love. But the poor sinner who glimpses that Love for a moment, and opens his or her heart to receive it, suddenly understands the otherwise incomprehensible meaning of the Gospel:

> And can it be that I should gain
> An interest in the Saviour's blood?
> Died he for me, who caused his pain?
> For me, who him to death pursued?
> Amazing love! how can it be
> That you, my God, should die for me?
>
> He left his Father's throne above,
> So free, so infinite his grace;
> Emptied himself of all but love,
> And bled for Adam's helpless race;
> 'Tis mercy all, immense and free;
> For, O my God, it found out me.

This is the Gospel, so full of joy and glory that it is intoxicating in its influence, as anyone who feels and knows the Wesleyan hymns (like the above) from the inside also understands. It is the same inebriating and liberating Gospel that filled the hearts and minds of believers in the early Church. This is not sermonizing about crowns of joy and glory, not 'pie in the sky when we die', not preaching so as to ameliorate the conditions of poverty and suffering in this life in order to keep suffering people quiet with promises of heaven hereafter. This Gospel so filled believers with the joy of forgiveness, and so baptized them with the Holy Spirit, that their minds and hearts were on fire with God, and they went singing out to die!

In Smyrna, men and women were undergoing the pressure of violent persecution, their world was one in which the drama of suffering, torture and martyrdom was being played out before their very eyes. But in the midst of it all the Gospel worked – the Saviour sustained his people, and the persecuting crowd were amazed with the praying, singing, rejoicing believers who, in the last hours of their lives on earth, beheld a vision of heaven, and sometimes, like the protomartyr Stephen, could cry out in dying anticipation: 'Look … I see the heavens opened and the Son of Man standing at the right hand of God!' (Acts 7:56).

*

Prayer

Lord Jesus, King of the Martyrs:

In life you are our forgiveness, joy and peace, and in death you are our hope and glory;

We praise you for all those who have lived and died in your love, and who have burned with the fierce and glorious fire of the Holy Spirit.

Grant us a dynamic faith like theirs, courage in our adversities, and joyful fellowship at last in the communion of saints. Amen.

*

Response

Look up all the crown references referred to in this meditation, and read the verses around them. Then read through the hymn

'O Sacred head ...' and ask in which way the Church in this country is suffering for preaching and living the truth of the Gospel.

If you feel there is no persecution and suffering ask the reason why. And what about your own life?

Then why not take up one of the suggestions in this morning's meditation? Amnesty International News (regular leaflet or cassette) can be received monthly from: Amnesty International, 1 Easton Street, London WC1X 8DJ.

*

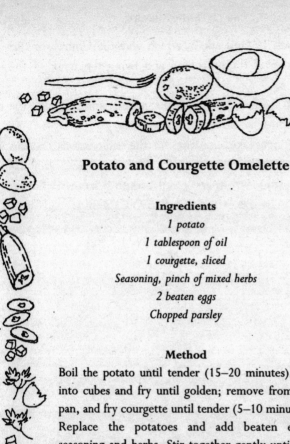

Potato and Courgette Omelette

Ingredients

1 potato
1 tablespoon of oil
1 courgette, sliced
Seasoning, pinch of mixed herbs
2 beaten eggs
Chopped parsley

Method

Boil the potato until tender (15–20 minutes), cut into cubes and fry until golden; remove from the pan, and fry courgette until tender (5–10 minutes). Replace the potatoes and add beaten eggs, seasoning and herbs. Stir together gently until the eggs set, turn and cook on the other side. Serve sprinkled with chopped parsley.

Pergamum

Letter to the Church at Pergamum

Revelation 2:12–17

And to the angel of the church in Pergamum write:

These are the words of him who has the sharp two-edged sword:

I know where you are living, where Satan's throne is. Yet you are holding fast to my name, and you did not deny your faith in me even in the days of Antipas my witness, my faithful one, who was killed among you, where Satan lives.

But I have a few things against you: you have some there who hold to the teaching of Balaam, who taught Balak to put a stumbling block before the people of Israel, so that they would eat food sacrificed to idols and practise fornication. So you also have some who hold to the teaching of the Nicolaitans.

Repent then. If not, I will come to you soon and make war against them with the sword of my mouth.

Let anyone who has an ear listen to what the Spirit is saying to the churches. To everyone who conquers I will give some of the hidden manna, and I will give a white stone, and on the white stone is written a new name that no one knows except the one who receives it.

The Throne of Satan:
The Church at Pergamum

The independent capital city Pergamum was willed to the
Roman empire by its last king, Attulis III in 133 BC. Rome
made it the capital of Asia Minor, and at the time of our text,
though it was not the commercial success that Ephesus and
Smyrna were, it remained the capital. R.H. Charles writes
of it:

> Pergamum was famed for its great religious foundations in
> honour of Zeus Soter, Athena Nikephoros, whose temple crowned
> the Acropolis, Dionysius Kathegmon, and Asklepios Soter. Of
> these the cult of Asklepios was the most distinctive and cel-
> ebrated. It was the Lourdes of the Province of Asia, and the seat
> of a famous school of medicine.

Situated geographically fifteen miles east of the Mediterranean,
and the third church on our journey of seven, it is the one
which has the dark distinction of being called the throne of
Satan. What is the reason for this?

Eight hundred feet up on Pergamum's conical hill, in front
of the temple of Athena, was built an altar to Zeus, on a great

projecting ledge, smoking with sacrifices to him. It actually looked like a huge throne on the mountainside.

Then with the worship of Asclepios, the god of healing, another reason for the title could be found. Galen, second only to the great physician Hippocrates, was born in Pergamum, and he said that people commonly swore by Asclepios Soter (Saviour) of Pergamum. This title challenged that of Jesus the Saviour of the world, and Asclepios' emblem was the serpent which could have indicated a satanic cult.

But for neither of these religious cults was the term 'the throne of Satan' reserved, for the old Greek gods had lost their power by this time, in the face of the state religion of Rome.

We have already seen in Smyrna that when religion is wedded to state and political policy it can become a very evil thing, and a totalitarianism can develop which claims the complete loyalty of human beings, body and soul. This has been the scourge of religious and secular history, responsible for bloodshed, massacre and the cruelties of inquisition and crusade, in the guise of Nazism, atheistic Marxism, and more subtly in the materialistic guise of international commercial conglomerates – the unacceptable face of capitalism.

Pergamum was the administrative capital, and the seat of the imperial cult. It was, therefore, the centre of that worship of the emperor where the burning of incense and the confession 'Caesar is Lord' was demanded on pain of death.

By this time, for John writing in Patmos, the emperors were the incarnation of Satan, and the centre of worship was his throne.

Remember the proconsul governor who challenged Polycarp in the stadium at Smyrna? He had the *ius gladii*, the power of the sword, and by it Polycarp was martyred. We have a named martyr here in Pergamum to whom we shall refer later, but any Christian in Pergamum lived under the sword's shadow.

In our text Christ also has the power of the sword, but this is the sword of the Spirit, and its light is greater than the state's darkness. There were eastern religions in which the powers of light and darkness were in eternal dualistic conflict, and it could not be affirmed that light would ultimately gain the victory. But there is no such dualism here. To live for Christ was an immense risk in worldly terms, but the Christian looked to the transcendent Pantocrator, in whose hands alone lay the ultimate issues of life and death. To live for Christ was joy, and to die was gain (Philippians 1:21).

The Christian was not to flee the city. Christ knew where the believers lived, and willed them to be in the world though not of the world system (John 17:15f.). The world can also be redeemed, and the kingdom of God can be expressed in good government, the *Pax Romana*, religious freedom, justice and medical care.

An illustration of this is found in the name Pergamum, for the word for *parchment* is derived from it, and this is how it came about. For centuries scrolls were written on papyrus, made of Egyptian bullrushes. The library at Pergamum was second only to that of Alexandria, and it contained about 200,000 parchment rolls. In the third century BC, Eumenes, the king of Pergamum, head-hunted Aristophanes the Alexandrian librarian for the library at Pergamum.

Ptolemy of Egypt, maddened by this act, imprisoned Aristophanes and forbade the export of papyrus to Pergamum. Faced with this embargo, Pergamum invented parchment or vellum, made of polished animal skins, and this eventually superseded papyrus. Such creative invention could be taken up into the purposes of God for the spread of truth in all its forms, and it was here, where the throne of Satan was set, that such creative invention could take place.

Day 3 Morning
Martyrdom and Heresy

Jesus said to the Ephesian church, 'I know your works'; to the Smyrnaean church, 'I know your afflictions'; and now he says to the Pergamum church, 'I know where you live'. This does not mean merely that he knew their geographical location, but that he knew the physical persecution, the psychological pressure, and the spiritual danger they were in. Christ's knowing was the guarantee of being held, sustained and undergirded by his compassion, with the power to overcome. Our 'situation' in this wider sense means that we cannot drift outside the sustaining love of God *if* we look to him in our need when surrounded by all that Satan can unleash against us. There is a real sense in which we cannot move outside his love, even if we wanted to, for 'if I make my bed in hell, you are there also' (Psalm 139:8). But we must not presume, for we are given clear commandment when surrounded by the sins of the world and the heresies of the Church:

> *Build yourselves up on your most holy faith; pray in the Holy Spirit; keep yourselves in the love of God; look forward to the mercy of our Lord Jesus Christ that leads to eternal life (Jude 20f.).*

When Christ tells us that he knows where we live, he does not expect us to settle down in our Pergamum, for we are strangers and pilgrims, sojourners on the earth (1 Peter 2:11; Hebrews 11:13). We are citizens of the kingdom of heaven and our time on earth should reflect the values, ethics and glories of that eternal kingdom (Philippians 3:20). This does not mean a withdrawal from society – indeed the opposite is true. The Christian does not have to be a party political animal, but he or she must bring Christian values to bear upon the life of society as a Christian member of it.

In a totalitarian state, or even in failing democracies, conflicts will arise between Church and state. If religion has become corrupt, then men and women of good will are those who will express the values of the kingdom of God, while corrupt religious and political people bent on profit and power will express the values of the kingdom of darkness. It is salutary to remember the national socialist church in Germany opposed by the underground Confessing Church; the Orthodox puppets in the Soviet Union opposed to the underground Orthodox and Baptist Churches; the religio/political machinery of apartheid in South Africa, confronted by Desmond Tutu and others.

We must never forget that Jesus himself was crucified by a combination of religious authorities and the state, and this is what he meant when he said:

If the world hates you, be aware that it hated me before it hated you. If you belonged to the world, the world would love you as its own. Because you do not belong to the world, but I have chosen you out of the world – therefore the world hates you (John 15:18f.).

The 'world' here is not, of course, the natural world of which we are the ecological guardians, nor the world where values of compassion and freedom are practised, but the 'world system' which is dedicated to money, power and sexual gratification for their own sake, and where one set of political strategists manipulates power over others.

In such situations Dietrich Bonhoeffer must oppose the Nazi system, Solzhenitsyn must witness against the Gulag archipelago, Nelson Mandela must suffer under apartheid, Thomas Merton must shout (as a Trappist!) against the Vietnam war and nuclear weapons, and Oscar Romero must suffer and die opposing right wing violence in El Salvador.

The political left and right have their extremes and abuses of power, and left to itself, the Church will persecute and inhibit religious freedom and tolerance. This is a world in which the throne of Satan is firmly placed, and it is religious as well as secular.

We have recorded some of the great names of our time, but today, as in the days of Pergamum, many heroes of faith are known to God alone outside their immediate circle. Antipas was one of these – Pergamum's martyr. It is interesting to note that the word *martus* may be translated *witness* or *martyr*. The translations vary, but the context demands *martyr* for Antipas who shed his blood for Christ. It was later that the distinction between martyrs and confessors was made.

In the New Testament, martyr and witness were the same, for certainly in the days of the Apocalypse it was expected that witnesses would become martyrs if they were faithful! The great joy is that Antipas is named 'my faithful martyr' by the Saviour, for that very title is Christ's in Revelation 1:5 and 3:14. He names his disciples with his own name and claims them as his own.

Then suddenly, after this commendation of Antipas, comes a word of rebuke and warning: 'I have a few things against you ...' (2:14). We come up against the names Balaam and

Nicolaitans. They are found also in Ephesus and Thyatira – pernicious heretical influences among the churches of God. This is not persecution from outside but corruption from within. There are some unedifying passages in Numbers 25:1–5; 31:16, which give a clue to the origin and content of the Balaam cult. Balaam is linked with encouraging immoral sexual and idolatrous religious practices between Israel and the people and gods of Moab – a linking of Yahweh with the fertility rites of the heathen. It exposes the danger in religious syncretism, and the mingling of undisciplined religion with the lure of easy sexual liaisons is an explosive mixture.

Some of the church fathers thought that the deacon Nicolaus (Acts 6:5) went morally and religiously wrong, while others blamed his interpreters, and they report sexual indulgence and heresy as the result. It is out of such a situation that the Council of Jerusalem counselled that the Gentiles were to abstain from things sacrificed to idols, and from sexual immorality (Acts 15:28f.).

The teaching among these people seems to have been that since Christians are not under law but under grace, they are free to do what they want. They may also have been infected with the teaching that since the body (the flesh) is evil, and only the 'spiritual' is important, you can use the body as you desire. These sort of teachings were in the New Testament as elements of later Gnosticism, and they corrupted the Church from within. Even when Paul was taking his leave of the Ephesian elders he foresaw such corruption and heresy:

I know that after I have gone, savage wolves will come in among
you, not sparing the flock. Some even from your own group will

*come distorting the truth in order to entice the disciples to follow
them. Therefore be alert (Acts 20:29–31).*

In our own days there is a 'pick'n'mix' mentality abroad which
operates in the moral and theological sphere in which both
Christian doctrine and morals are relative. This leads to a laid-
back attitude towards the great truths of our faith and a loss of
standards, leaving young Christians bewildered and unprepared
when faced with the immoralities and ideologies of our world.

It does matter what and how we believe, and it is necessary for
us to live upright and integrated lives. If this is done within the
fellowship of Christ then the result will be stability and maturity
within ourselves, and an overflow of compassion and hope in our
world. In this way we shall be faithful witnesses to the truth and
joy of the Gospel, and become lights that shine in a dark world.

*

Prayer

Lord Jesus, to whom all hearts are open:

*You have redeemed your people and sustained them in times of suffering
and persecution;*

*You have warned your Church of the world systems of power, manipu-
lation and violence;*

*Grant that we may give our minds and hands to men and women of
compassion, and in spite of all opposition work for truth, justice
and love;*

*Thus, keeping ourselves within the love of God, may our hearts await
your coming in glory, when the kingdoms of our world shall come
under your joyous and gentle rule.   Amen.*

*

Response

Are you aware of the suffering and victorious Church in other lands?

Do you participate in the missionary work of your church?

Get to know the missionary society your church supports, read its magazine, and resolve to get to know specific missionaries, especially in difficult areas, and pray for them methodically and regularly. Why not write to a particular missionary and pledge some other support?

*

Day 3 Evening
Christ's Two-edged Sword

This morning we concluded by hearing the substance of Christ's rebuke against doctrinal heresy and immoral practices. In our own day, in a society which has lost ultimate values and rejects authority, we must be careful not to swing to the other extreme and become fundamentalist in our knowledge of what is absolutely correct to believe or absolutely moral in the way we live. We do not live and die by legalisms but by the gracious and spontaneous participation in the life of God which overflows in love and generosity.

The Church of God has been given the immense gift of the revelation of God in Jesus Christ which is enshrined in the scriptures, and is maintained in truth by the free grace of the Holy Spirit. That does not mean that the Church or the Bible is infallible. We must be able to differentiate between the words *authoritative* and *infallible* – they are not synonymous.

If we cling to and preach our infallibilities we shall paint ourselves into a corner and be unable to reach the world in which there is a mixture of lostness and compassion, and in which we should be immersed in order that Christ's light may shine.

There have been times when the Church, following the example of the state, has used the power of the sword to maintain authority and keep the flock in what it saw as doctrinal orthodoxy. An orthodoxy of doctrine and practice that relies on the power of the sword for its maintenance has nothing to do with faith in Christ, and is no better than toeing the party line in fear of punishment.

Both the Reformed and Catholic sections of the Church have been responsible for such fundamentalisms, and this has alienated some of the world's best minds and hearts — and continues to do so. We should rather hold to St Augustine's dictum: 'In things essential, unity; in things non-essential, liberty; in all things, charity.'

In the light of these thoughts we turn to Christ's use of the two-edged sword. First of all, let us be clear as to what it is *not*. During my years in Zurich I often looked up with sorrow at the powerful statue of the Swiss reformer Zwingli, near the Grossminster and the river Limmat where he drowned Anabaptists because they would not conform to his vision of what the Church should be. He stood there straight and severe, holding a Bible in his hand and leaning upon a long and threatening sword, representing the spiritual and secular swords of scripture and punishment. Zwingli was killed on the field of Capel fighting a Catholic army, and Luther's comment was that he died under judgement for fighting a spiritual battle with carnal weapons. It is easy for us to stand in judgement outside such situations — remember that Luther himself became engaged in violent warfare against the peasants ten years later, in fear of political and moral anarchy.

For my part, I admire the pre-Constantinian Church in which Christians did not take up arms or engage in warfare, and I long for the Church of Christ to be pacifist in our contemporary world. But I also realize that the problems of living as citizens of this world and of the kingdom of God are immense. And in any case, it was not a pacifist ideology which moved the early Church, but the will and love of the Prince of Peace.

So what is this two-edged sword? 'I will make war against them,' says Christ, 'with the sword of my mouth' (2:16). Remember that Balaam himself was confronted by an angel with a drawn sword (Numbers 22:23). The donkey saw the vision but Balaam did not, and insisted on beating the donkey because he was too dull to understand the animal's discernment!

We are not to base our ethical stance on the books of Numbers or Joshua (see Numbers 31:8; Joshua 8:22), but note that the angel's sword in the Balaam story was the sword of the prophetic word. The New Testament is clear that the sword of Christ is his word, and it is by such gospel proclamation that the Church is to engage in spiritual warfare:

The word of God is living and active, sharper than any two-edged sword, piercing until it divides soul from spirit, joints from marrow; it is able to judge the thoughts and intentions of the heart (Hebrews 4:12).

The sword of the Spirit with which we are to stand against the evil world and demonic powers is the word of God (Ephesians 6:17). And even were some to argue that God's will is ultimately brought about by the fall of wicked nations and ideologies, we must not take up the sword in the name of Christ and profess to be 'the arm of the Lord' in retribution. This has been the bane of the three Abrahamic faiths in holy wars, jihads and crusades.

Never take revenge, my friends, but instead let God's anger do it. For the scripture says, 'I will take revenge, I will pay back, says the Lord.' Instead, as the scripture says: 'If your enemies are hungry, feed them, if they are thirsty, give them a drink; for by doing this you will make them burn with shame.' Do not let evil defeat you; instead, conquer evil with good (Romans 12:19–21; GNB).

The last word to the Pergamum believers is not a word of judgement but of encouragement, sustenance and promise. Whatever we feel about the sorrows, compromises and involvement of Church and world, we must affirm that the last word is with the mercy and love of God. After all, it is not we who shall ultimately put personal or international wrongs to right, for we cannot bring in the kingdom of God. The initiative and the consummation rest with the One who is called Pantocrator, the Almighty.

This last word is twofold, consisting of hidden manna and a mysterious white stone, and interpretations abound.

First, hidden manna. The very word is derived by folk etymology from *man hu* ('What is it?'). The story is told in Exodus 16:11–15, where the Lord provided Israel with a strange new food in the wilderness. When they saw it they asked: 'What is it?' and from that question the name *manna* was derived – a heavenly food of God's provision.

A pot of this manna was placed in the ark of the covenant in the tabernacle, and later in Solomon's Temple. Swete's commentary tells the story (from 2 Maccabees 2:5ff. and elsewhere) that at the destruction of the temple in the sixth century Jeremiah hid the pot of manna and the ark in a cave on Mount Sinai, sealing it secretly. It would be discovered on the return of the Messiah, and to eat of the hidden manna would be to enjoy the presence of Messiah.

In the psalter it is called 'the bread of angels' (78:24f.), *panis angelicus*, which brings us to a liturgical reference to the Christian eucharist, for Jesus is the bread of life (John 6:31–35), the hidden manna. Jesus picks up the story of manna in the wilderness and applies it directly to himself, as a fulfilment of the Mosaic provision, and as a foretaste of the heavenly banquet:

> *I am the bread of life. Whoever comes to me will never be hungry, and whoever believes in me will never be thirsty (John 6:35).*

Those who feed on Christ the hidden manna lose their taste for food offered to idols, for 'you cannot partake of the table of the Lord and the table of demons' (1 Corinthians 10:21).

Then the white stone with the new name. R.H. Charles in his commentary lists various interpretations which have been employed to understand this mysterious token:

* a white stone was given by jurors to signify absolution and aquittal;
* to admit to a royal assembly or religious feast;
* rabbinic tradition claims that white stones fell with the manna in the wilderness;
* it is associated with the inscribed stones upon the breastplate of the high priest (Exodus 28:29f.), and may have been a hidden diamond inscribed with the sacred tetragrammaton – the four sacred letters YHWH, the name of Yahweh;
* it is related to the presentation of a white stone as a token of felicity.

But the most likely interpretation is the custom, in the ancient world, of carrying a stone amulet or charm engraved with a sacred or god's name. To know the name was to have power, to call upon the god in time of need, to be held in an aura of protection. In the promise to Pergamum the stone was white, the colour of holiness in the Apocalypse, and the new name was the baptismal name of the believer in the image of Christ.

Our line-drawing illustration for Pergamum shows the name of the martyr Antipas upon the white stone. We have seen that Antipas was named with the name of Christ, the faithful witness and martyr, but only the one who receives the stone can know the secret of the name which God gives. God alone knows the potential of his image in my own soul, that mysterious secret he reveals to me over the years of my sanctification and pilgrimage, and its fullness will only be revealed when all mirrored reflections will be done away and we shall behold Christ's glory face to face (1 Corinthians 13:12).

Abram became Abraham (Genesis 17:5), Jacob became Israel (Genesis 32:28); Simon became Peter (Matthew 16:17f.). With the new name there is a new birth, a new song, a new Jerusalem and a new heaven and earth, for in the believer God makes all things new (Revelation 21:5).

*

Prayer

Lord Christ, Living Word of the Father:

Your two-edged sword has pierced my heart, for I have not lived faithfully, or loved wholeheartedly;

In times of conflict I have run to hide, and when your truth has been challenged I have compromised my conscience.

Let me now embrace the discipline of repentance and restoration, grant me healing by the wounds of your love, and admit me to taste the hidden manna of your new life.   Amen.

*

Response

Many Christians are drawn to the life and example of a particular saint of God in sacred history or in the contemporary Church. The believers in Pergamum saw the martyr Antipas as reflecting the suffering and joy of Christ, and modelled their lives on his.

Why not choose a man or woman of faith, read their story and ask what light they throw upon your own spirituality and discipleship?

*

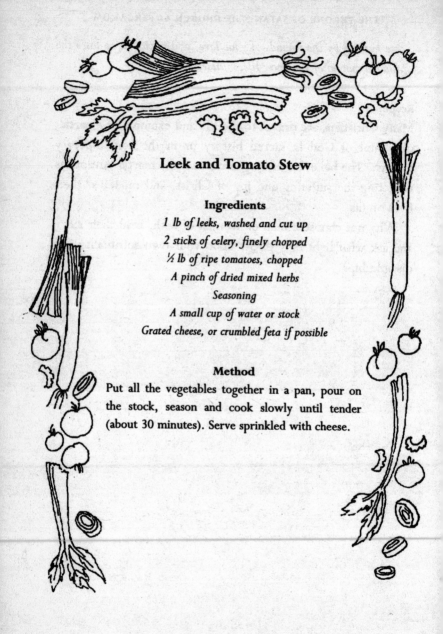

Leek and Tomato Stew

Ingredients

1 lb of leeks, washed and cut up
2 sticks of celery, finely chopped
½ lb of ripe tomatoes, chopped
A pinch of dried mixed herbs
Seasoning
A small cup of water or stock
Grated cheese, or crumbled feta if possible

Method

Put all the vegetables together in a pan, pour on the stock, season and cook slowly until tender (about 30 minutes). Serve sprinkled with cheese.

Thyatira, gateway to Pergamum

Thyatira

Letter to the Church at Thyatira

Revelation 2:18–29

And to the angel of the church in Thyatira write:

These are the words of the Son of God, who has eyes like a flame of fire, and whose feet are like burnished bronze:

I know your works — your love, faith, service and patient endurance. I know that your last works are greater than the first. But I have this against you: you tolerate that woman Jezebel, who calls herself a prophet and is teaching and beguiling my servants to practise fornication and to eat food sacrificed to idols. I gave her time to repent, but she refuses to repent of her fornication. Beware, I am throwing her on a bed, and those who commit adultery with her I am throwing into great distress, unless they repent of her doings; and I will strike her children dead. And all the churches will know that I am the one who searches minds and hearts, and I will give to each of you as your works deserve.

But to the rest of you in Thyatira, who do not hold this teaching, who have not learned what some call 'the deep things of Satan', to you I say, I do not lay on you any other burden; only hold fast to what you have until I come.

To everyone who conquers and continues to do my works to the end, I will give authority over the nations; to rule them with an iron rod, as when clay pots are shattered — even as I also received authority from my Father.

To the one who conquers I will also give the morning star. Let anyone who has an ear listen to what the Spirit is saying to the churches.

The Danger of Compromise: The Church at Thyatira

The circuit now turns south. We began at Ephesus, then north to Smyrna and Pergamum. Now the southern road runs through Thyatira and on to Sardis and Laodicea. It was the imperial post road, filled with commerce, so that although Thyatira was the least important of the seven cities, it was a prosperous commercial town, and the gateway to Pergamum, the capital. For that reason it had an armed garrison of Macedonian troops as a delaying action protecting the capital, though lacking a fortified height it could only delay a concentrated attack.

Thyatira itself did not pose a secular or religious threat to the church there, as it was a centre for neither. It had a female oracle called Sambathé with its fortune-telling shrine, and a tutelary divinity Apollo Tyrimnaios, but neither of these was a real threat to the church.

It was named Thyatira by Seleucus Nicator after the conquest of Persia by Alexander, and came into Roman hands in 190 BC. It was famous chiefly for the flourishing dyeing industry; it is significant that Lydia of the Macedonian city of Philippi belonged to the dyeing guild (Acts 16:14f.). Among the seven, we know least about Thyatira but the trade in woollen and dyed goods, and various inscriptions, witness to the powerful trade guilds established there. They existed for profit and pleasure, and extended also to workers in leather, linen, bronze, pottery, bakery and the slave trade. Here lay the chief problem for the Christians of Thyatira – that of commercial compromise.

It was not simply a matter of joining the trade union, but also meant involvement in the pagan temple in which meetings were held, a formal sacrifice to the gods and the consuming of meat which had been offered to idols. Sometimes, too, these communal meals would degenerate into drunkenness and immorality.

The problem seems to be that a 'Jezebel woman' had influence in the church at Thyatira, and like her counterpart after whom she was named (1 Kings 16:31), she exercised the power of a prophetess, and so arose the religious syncretism which linked Yahweh with Baal for the sake of commercial profit. The judgement spoken to Thyatira by Christ was carried out, for Epiphanius tells us that it became a centre for the heresy of Montanism,* and ceased to exist towards the close of the second century.

*A prophetic movement which amongst other things, incurred the hostility of church leaders by its ecstatic manner of utterance, the unusual prominence of women, and an asceticism which often disrupted marriages.

Day 4 Morning
A Corrupted Faith

Faith may be corrupted not only by attacks from heathenism and persecution from without, but subtly from compromise of doctrine and practice from within. Such was the case at Thyatira, and 'that Jezebel woman' (Moffat) was the cause.

There were false prophets at Ephesus and Pergamum, but here it was a false prophetess, and it is significant that the heresy of Montanism later flourished in Thyatira, with its prophetesses Prisca and Maximilla claiming to be mouthpieces of the Holy Spirit.

These are days when the ministry of women in the Church is at last being valued and appreciated as never before, and it is important for us to recognize at this point the difference between two women of Thyatira – Lydia and Jezebel. There was a cultural and pastoral reticence to accept authoritative positions for women in the early Church, but in both the Old and New Testaments there were prophetesses who were vehicles of the word of God.

In the Old Testament we read of Miriam (Exodus 15:20), Deborah (Judges 4:4) and Huldah (2 Kings 22:14). In the New Testament appears that wonderful contemplative prophetess Anna (Luke 2:36), and the four virgin prophetesses who were daughters of Philip (Acts 21:9), as well as the women deacons and workers who laboured with Paul (Romans 16:1, 3, 6; 1 Corinthians 16:19; Colossians 4:15).

So it was not because she claimed to be a prophetess that this woman was condemned but because she was a 'Jezebel', corrupting both faith and practice among the people of God.

With such a name we must look at the original Jezebel as a clue to her influence in Thyatira. Queen Jezebel was the daughter of Ethbaal, king of Sidon, and her story is told in the First Book of Kings. She married Ahab, king of Israel, and she brought into the kingdom the god Baal and the goddess Asherah, with a temple in Samaria. She advocated a mixture of Baal-Yahweh religion, which included murder, harlotry and witchcraft (1 Kings 21:14; 2 Kings 9:22). That kind of evil compromise led to actual apostasy, bad religion leading to wholesale corruption, and a blunting of both spiritual and moral sense. This is possible in all parts of Christ's Church – both then and now:

> Now the Spirit expressly says that in later times some will renounce the faith by paying attention to deceitful spirits and teachings of demons, through the hypocrisy of liars whose consciences are seared with a hot iron (1 Timothy 4:1–2).

Morals cannot be separated from religion, and a religion which has become corrupted leads to a blunting of moral sense. There are ancient and modern examples where charismatic religious charlatans are linked with sexual corruption and promiscuity, and where money and power loom large in their lifestyle.

Yet it is not only *corrupt* religion that leads to corruption of life – *any* religion degenerates when wedded to establishment and power structures. It may be simplistic to say that the trouble began when the emperor Constantine claimed to have a vision or dream of the cross of Christ emblazoned on his soldier's shield in AD 313, but certainly it was a subtle political move in the unification of the empire. The accounts vary, but this was a watershed, the beginnings of a politically accepted and established church, raised from a persecuted to a favoured status. Was this the beginning of a politicized and castrated religion, or the end of a schismatic sect and the beginning of a universal catholic Church?

Within our Franciscan community we have various attitudes toward the infamous Brother Elias who compromised the vision of St Francis of Assisi, yet whose work and influence was the watershed for Franciscanism – for good or ill?

In both cases there are those who mourn over a pristine vision compromised, when purity was exchanged for power structures of the established and secular culture, and it became easier, more acceptable and reasonable to accommodate the vision.

The primitive vision is radical, but there is always a Judas among the twelve, a Jezebel within the community, a Constantine waiting for an instrument of political unity, an Elias to reinterpret the early Franciscan vision.

If we look at our own religious church or denomination (and I write as an ecumenical Christian), we can find compromise, corruption, double-dealing and double-think. If we look within our own hearts it is there too – that principle of accommodation, compromise, laxity, which betrays the vocation to utmost dedication. I recall the breath-taking recognition of challenge when I first read the poem 'The Call' by Father Andrew SDC:

> *My friend, beware of me*
> *Lest I should do*
> *The very thing I'd sooner die than do,*
> *In some way crucify the Christ in you.*

If you are called to some great sacrifice,
And I should come to you with frightened eyes
And cry, 'Take care, take care, be wise, be wise!'
See through my softness, then a fiend's attack,
And bid me get straight behind your back;
To your own conscience and your God be true
Lest I play Satan to the Christ in you.

And I would humbly ask of you in turn
That if some day in me Love's fires should burn
To whiteness, and a Voice should call
Bidding me leave my little for God's all,
If need be, you would thrust me from your side —
So keep love loyal to the Crucified.

So let us turn for the last moments of our meditation to that other woman from Thyatira — Lydia the seller of purple cloth whom we meet in Acts 16:14, 40.

She was among the 'God-fearers', a gentile patron of Jewish worship who gathered at the riverside in Philippi for sabbath prayers because there was no synagogue there. Paul and his companions were drawn there and joined in the prayer and exposition of scripture. Paul gave witness to Christ as messiah and Saviour, and preached the good news of forgiveness and love, as a result of which 'the Lord opened her heart to listen eagerly to what was said by Paul' (v. 14), and she was baptized with all her household into the community of faith.

Here is a wonderful example of the initiative of God following upon the proclamation of Christ. Lydia manifests a listening heart which becomes an open heart and results in an hospitable heart: 'If you have judged me to be faithful to the Lord, come and stay at my home.' And Luke, writing up the story, says, 'And she prevailed upon us.' She was immediately tested, for between her conversion and those last words, Paul and Silas were arrested, flogged and imprisoned for the faith – but she stuck by them.

Two women from Thyatira – a Jezebel and a Lydia – one whose early faith was compromised and whose influence led to schism with pernicious doctrinal and ethical corruption, and the other who is perpetuated in scripture with words of openness, simplicity and warm hospitality because of a saving experience of Christ. Our own situation is rarely black or white, but where do we stand today?

*

Prayer

Lord Jesus, Saviour and Judge:

Enable me to look into my own heart today, and see where early faith has been compromised, and where eager dedication has been tarnished by accommodation to secular values;

Lead me to repentance, and grant me again a listening heart, opened by your Holy Spirit to the reception of a new vision of God, a new enthusiasm in discipleship, and a new fellowship in my worshipping community. Amen.

*

Response

Can you see the difference between a *syncretism* which accommodates and adulterates Christian doctrine and morals, and a *synthesism* which joins all men and women of other faiths with common love for God and humankind?

Can you retain an openness of heart to all such people with

a clear affirmation of the uniqueness of Christ?

And can you also affirm the light of Christ shining in the best of other world faiths? Is this compromise or openness of heart?

Share such prayerful thinking with others who are on a contemplative path.

*

Day 4 Evening
Hold Fast!

We have been thinking about the baneful influence of a false prophetess in Thyatira, but we must also be aware of Christ's positive commendations. In linking the description of Christ in the earlier vision and in the present text we find him referred to as the Son of Man (1:13) and the Son of God (2:18). His appearance, with eyes like a flame of fire, and feet like burnished bronze, is suggested by Daniel 10:6 and Ezekiel 1:27, and in both places we have a mingling of judgement with a view to mercy. The all-seeing eyes of fire pierce through the veils of hypocrisy, and the feet of burnished bronze are ready to tread down the corrupting influences within the Church and the human heart.

We who have domesticated a 'gentle Jesus meek and mild' are suddenly confronted with the flashing of the divine judgement, and it reduces us to a trembling paralysis, as it did John the Divine and Daniel:

> I was left alone to see this great vision. My strength left me, and my complexion grew deathly pale, and I retained no strength ... and when I heard the sound of his words, I fell into a trance, face to the ground (Daniel 10:8f.).

The Christ revealed to us in the Pantocrator image of the Apocalypse is One who challenges us with the purity of his demands for righteousness. This figure is far removed from the subjective projections of nineteenth-century liberal theologians. They endeavoured to separate the Jesus of history from the Christ of faith, a task which foundered under the weight of the later and better biblical scholarship, for their benevolent but weak paternal father figure and their sentimental folk-Jesus was a far cry from the God of revelation.

The Pantocrator Christ was no soft imaginary figure invented by the needy psyche, though there is a kind of religion which projects a protective father figure or a brother Jesus figure, just as a child will project an imaginary playmate. And when a Freud or a Marx accuses such people of using religion as an opium or a crutch when they cannot face up to the grim realities of our human dilemma, they are right.

In the New Testament we have the opposite – a Christ who confronts us with an inflexible judgement, who demands righteousness, equity and a style of life which calls forth courage and adventure, the result of which fills the world with justice and compassion. This is the Christ who meets us in our text.

The beginning of the letter to Thyatira shows him to prefer mercy to judgement, and before it launches into the necessary rebuke of heresy and corruption there is the commendation of the virtues of the major part of the Thyatiran church. The fiery judgement of the God of revelation is the other side of the coin which shows sustaining mercy, for his retribution is but the outshining of his love. This means that God does not lose his temper, does not indulge in penal retribution which is simply revenge. His judgements are always for discipline and correction, and to such a God the sinner can always submit himself in fearful trust.

There is fire, but it is a refining fire, a purifying element that burns out the dross and purifies the metal, so that it glows with glory and reflects the image of the refiner.

This is why, after commending the believers for the vertical and horizontal virtues of love, faith, service and patient endurance, and after telling them that they have increased in such spiritual growth, he then faces them with the steady eye of judgement: 'But I have this against you ...' and then the whole internal and schismatic problem of 'that Jezebel woman' is laid before them.

A careful reading of the text shows that Christ encapsulates this false teaching, differentiating between this heretical group and the faithful ones who constitute the main body of believers. The severity of the description and condemnation is in order that an easy toleration may not lead to the infection of the spread of the heresy.

This is a contemporary problem. There is a line to be drawn between heresy and truth, between purity and immorality. On the one hand we must realize that the Church is a hospital for sinners and not a hotel for saints, and we ought not to draw ourselves together in a holy huddle, pretending to be a pure, gathered Church – clean, holy and untouchable. But on the other hand if we name the name of Christ we must depart from evil (2 Timothy 2:19).

There must be compassion, warmth, understanding, forgiveness and a helping hand stretched out to all who are caught up in the sins and sorrows of our world. Christ's openness to prostitutes, tax-gatherers, lepers and sinners of every hue is the attitude and atmosphere which should mark a New Testament Church. So where is the line drawn? How does one differentiate between open, compassionate welcome and toleration of sin and heresy?

Paul Tillich has a telling exposition of the dilemma of the

Reformers Luther, Zwingli and Calvin when they had to choose between the ecclesiastical type of church and the sectarian type of the evangelical radicals. We sometimes make this distinction in speaking of a 'folk-church' over against a 'gathered church', and there are mixtures of both in our mainline denominations. But it is worth recording Tillich's words in *A History of Christian Thought*:

> The ecclesiastical type of church is the mother from which we come. It is always there and we belong to it from birth; we did not choose it. When we awaken out of the dimness of the early stages of life, we can then perhaps reaffirm that we belong to it in confirmation, but we already belong to it objectively. This is quite different from the churches of the radical enthusiasts, where the individual who decides that he wants to be a member of the church is the creative power of the church. The church is made by a covenant through the decision of individuals to form a church, an assembly of God. Everything here is dependent on the independent individual, who is not born from the mother church, but who creates active church communities.

Depending upon our upbringing, our reading of scripture and our own church tradition, we will find ourselves preferring one type to another, and there is a mixture of both in the New Testament. The sectarian type tends to desire a pure community, exercising strong discipline and excommunicating those who do not toe the line in doctrine or morals, while the ecclesiastical type tends to desire a church which embraces sinners while acknowledging the evangelical counsels of perfection.

This dilemma was present in certain ways in the early

Church, and one of the things that affected both the Corinthian church and the Thyatiran church was the problem of eating meat which had been offered to idols, for this was a theological as well as a moral problem.

Notice that the solution seems to have been different within the differing atmosphere of Corinth about AD 55 and Thyatira AD 95. The situation and argument is well set out in 1 Corinthians 8–10, where Paul says that on the one hand pagan gods have no objective reality, so there is no difference in offered or non-offered meats, but on the other hand many believers felt that to eat such meat was to eat at the table of demons, and to participate in the ritual of paganism.

Paul acknowledged that if such meat is tainted by demonic influence, then that puts a different aspect on the matter. So he says that it doesn't really matter one way or the other, but then he reaches the pastoral solution of not partaking because of the arguments, consciences and attitudes of some brothers and sisters.

In the case of Thyatira, as a member of a trade guild, Jezebel seems not only to be willing to join in the communal guild meal in the pagan temple, with formal offering to the god, but also to tolerate, for the sake of commercial interests, the ensuing drunkenness and revelry.

There also seems something more sinister involved here, for the Christ, apart from Jezebel's immorality and participation in paganism, speaks of a teaching described as 'the deep things of Satan'.

It is difficult to know what is referred to, and it may well be a reference to the technical terms which were already being used in the early Church. Gnosticism had not flowered at this time, but already there were those who were speaking of *gnosis* (knowledge) of mysteries which were an addition, or even a substitute, for the simplicity of Christ, and which gave one admittance to the deep and hidden nature of the mystery of God.

Paul had already written to the nearby church at Colossae which seemed caught up in an early variety of Gnosticism, and warned them:

> See to it that no one takes you captive through philosophy and empty deceit, according to human tradition, according to the elemental spirits of the universe, and not according to Christ. For in him the whole fullness of deity dwells bodily, and you have come to fullness in him, who is the head of every ruler and authority. (Colossians 2:8–10).

The true *gnosis* or knowledge of God for the believer is to know Christ (John 17:3), and the deep things of God are revealed to the believer in Christ by the Holy Spirit (1 Corinthians 2:9–11)

There is a true Christian contemplative orientation, but there is also a contemplation of evil, the depths of Satan. The lure of dark and esoteric knowledge is only a real temptation to those who are capable of a contemplative dimension. Here, then, is a warning that the search for a contemplative vision which is not of God can lead a soul, or a church, into dark and esoteric ways in which heresy and immorality lead to a final condemnation. This is the point at which Christ cried out: 'Hold fast!'

It is a rallying call back to the basic teaching of repentance towards God and faith in Jesus Christ; to the acknowledgement of human sinfulness and trust in divine grace for salvation; and back to the indwelling power of the Holy Spirit as the means of inward love towards God and humankind. These are the things to which the believer and the Church must hold fast.

The letter ends with the promise of reward, and that reward is the fullness of Christ himself: 'To the one who conquers I will also give the morning star.' In the final chapter of Revelation Jesus' last word to the seven churches is: 'I am the Alpha and the Omega ... the root and the descendant of David, the bright morning star' (22:12, 16).

This is the light that shall never fail, the life that shall never cease, the love that shall never end.

*

Prayer

Jesus, Bright and Morning Star:

Your radiance warms and enlightens my life, clarifies my motivation and shines upon the path of my vocation;

Your eyes flame with loving judgement, and your voice calls me back to a renewal of love.

What can I do but raise to you my listening heart, and wait for the life-giving touch of your Holy Spirit?   Amen.

*

Response

Test your sensitivity and openness of heart and mind to all kinds of people who should be welcomed into your life and into your church.

What kinds would not be welcome? Why not?

Do you limit the welcome and love of Christ to any?

What are you going to do about it?

*

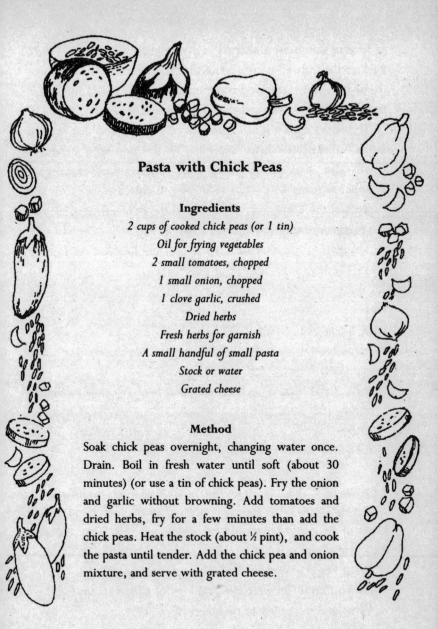

Pasta with Chick Peas

Ingredients

2 cups of cooked chick peas (or 1 tin)
Oil for frying vegetables
2 small tomatoes, chopped
1 small onion, chopped
1 clove garlic, crushed
Dried herbs
Fresh herbs for garnish
A small handful of small pasta
Stock or water
Grated cheese

Method

Soak chick peas overnight, changing water once. Drain. Boil in fresh water until soft (about 30 minutes) (or use a tin of chick peas). Fry the onion and garlic without browning. Add tomatoes and dried herbs, fry for a few minutes than add the chick peas. Heat the stock (about ½ pint), and cook the pasta until tender. Add the chick pea and onion mixture, and serve with grated cheese.

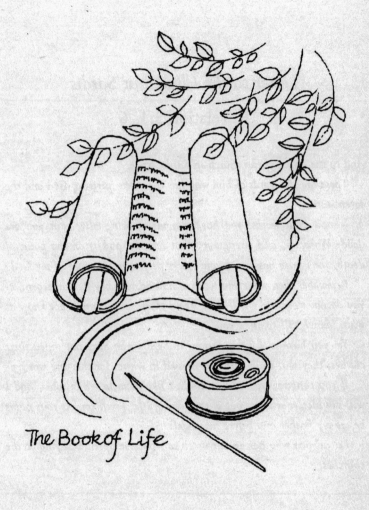

The Book of Life

Sardis

Letter to the Church at Sardis

Revelation 3:1–6

And to the angel of the church in Sardis write:

These are the words of him who has the seven spirits of God and the seven stars.

I know your works; you have a name of being alive, but you are dead. Wake up, and strengthen what remains and is on the point of death, for I have not found your works perfect in the sight of my God.

Remember then what you received and heard; obey it, and repent. If you do not wake up, I will come like a thief, and you will not know at what hour I will come to you.

Yet you have still a few persons in Sardis who have not soiled their clothes; they will walk with me, dressed in white, for they are worthy.

If you conquer, you will be clothed like them in white robes, and I will not blot your name out of the book of life; I will confess your name before my Father and before his angels.

Let anyone who has an ear listen to what the Spirit is saying to the churches.

Dead or Alive?
The Church at Sardis

Sardis, city of degeneration, torpor and morbidity. Standing on the trade road, thirty miles south of Thyatira on the way to Philadelphia, between the river Hermus and Mount Tmolus, it had been, in turn, Lydian, Persian, Greek and Roman, and had been celebrated for its wealth like its last Lydian king, Croesus, c. 560 BC.

The original Sardis was a plural noun, *Sardeis*, because there were two towns, the original on the Tmolus plateau and one spread in the valley below. The gold-bearing river Pactolus flowed through the city, but its chief source of wealth was its trade.

King Croesus provides a parable of Sardis, for he did not discern the seeds of degeneration or understand when the wise Solon warned him: 'Call no man happy until he is dead.' Croesus was warned again before he went to war with Cyrus of Persia, for he went for counsel to the famous oracle at Delphi, and was told: 'If you cross the river Halys, you will destroy a great empire.' But the prophecy was against himself. Even when he fled in defeat back to his impregnable citadel in Sardis, he did not ensure a guard upon the battlements, and the city fell.

Sardis later became a Greek city under Alexander the Great, but after his death, in a battle of rivals, the battlements were again left unguarded, and a band of men climbed the cliffs and took the city because Sardis was not on the watch.

Then came the Romans. It was not the fault of Sardis when an earthquake decimated it in AD 17, and the emperor bailed it out by donating ten million sisterces and remitted taxes for five years — an easy way out. There was a revival of the woollen and dyeing industry, and soon Sardis was wealthy but flabby again. This seems to be the spiritual story of the Sardian church. As Plummer writes:

> The church in Sardis has no Nicolaitans, no Balaam, no Jezebel. But there is worse evil than the presence of what is morally and doctrinally corrupt. The numbness of spiritual torpor and death is more hopeless than unwise toleration. The church in Sardis, scarcely out of its infancy, has already the signs of an effete and moribund faith; and it is possible that this deadness was a result of the absence of internal enemies.

Day 5 Morning
Professing not Possessing

Here, in Sardis, we have a church which is nominally Christian but spiritually dead; professing to know, to love, to serve God, but possessing little of the inward marks of the Gospel. Hypocrisy is rife, and the spiritual story of Sardis reflects the lack of watchfulness which, in its history, allowed the city to be conquered and ransacked.

One of the intriguing things about writing as an ecumenical Christian is that you are able, sometimes, from a relatively objective vantage point, to see the different shades and hues of vanity and hypocrisy that infect different communions of the Church of Christ – especially your own!

It often happens that in a strong, centrally governed denomination, less account is taken of individual needs, and theological orthodoxy overrides pastoral care. But in denominations or groupings which boast of their independence, the unity of the body is in danger, and in rejecting a monarchical pope everyone becomes pope!

The point I am making is that though our hypocrisies are different, they are nevertheless real, and there are numerous ways in which the name to be alive is maintained when the inward reality has decayed.

Religious Orders are like that too, and the Franciscan story abounds in inward deadness being exposed for what it is.

One day St Francis visited a certain friary where a brother of great reputation lived. Outwardly he exhibited a sincere and holy life, praying day and night and maintaining complete silence. The other friars admired and praised him, and when he made his confession it was with signs and not words.

When Francis met him, he looked into the friar's soul, and discerned not only that his spirituality was a façade, but that inwardly he was eaten up with pride and spiritual wickedness.

Francis said nothing at first, but when the Minister General praised the friar for his influence and holiness, Francis simply and clearly said that the man was led away and deceived by a wicked spirit.

The Minister General was amazed and said that it was incredible that a friar of such reputation for good works could be such a hypocrite.

'Test him by telling him to confess his sins in Chapter,' said Francis. 'If he refuses to obey, you will know that what I have said is true.'

The implication, as the story is told in *The Mirror of Perfection*, is that the friar had felt the burning discernment of Francis on their first meeting, so when the Minister put him under obedience to confess in Chapter, he put his fingers to his lips, shook his head and showed by signs that he was not willing to do so because of his love of holy silence!

The Minister was a bit afraid of him, so let him go. But some days later the friar made off, leaving his habit behind him.

The story doesn't stop there, for it goes on to say that when two friars met him on the road some time later, they felt sorry for the man who was walking alone. But when they spoke to him about his former way of life, he turned away from them with swearing and cursing.

In this case, a reputation for spirituality and holiness was the conceit of the friar, and it was maintained by silence. Like

Sardis, the friar had carefully erected a hypocritical façade of spirituality, and the pretence was only exposed when he was confronted with real holiness coupled with down-to-earth discernment.

Our hypocrisies as churches and individuals may be of a different kind, but they always undermine the true nature of the Church of God, and the more spiritual they appear the more corrosive is the underlying decay. I am at present receiving replies to a Questionnaire I have sent out to Christian and non-Christian friends, and one that arrived this week reads:

> *Christians proclaim Good News of freedom and new life through Christ. Why then do I feel so unimpressed with so many who call themselves Christians? I'd like to be a Christian, however many churchgoers put me off. What do you think?*

What do I think? Well I think it is another case of Sardis: 'I know your works; you have a name of being alive, but you are dead.' Our churches, of all denominations, are filled with religionists who are not truly Christians, professing life but not possessing it, and their membership is that of a religious club.

This applies as much, perhaps even more, to vociferous, zealous and doctrinally motivated people who know the Bible and can talk theology, as it does to those who use the church and religion socially and aesthetically without a true knowledge of scripture or a saving experience of Christ.

Hypocrisies vary, but if the love of God, the compassion of Christ and the fire of the Holy Spirit is not pulsating in the life of the Church and of the believer, then it is nominal religion and not living faith.

What is the remedy? Christ set before Sardis the possibility of recovery:

- Wake up!
- Remember!
- Repent!
- Obey!

They are stark words, but the disease is mortal and the surgeon plies his scalpel radically. It is no use sticking a plaster over a suppurating wound. The poison needs to be evacuated and a course of powerful antibiotics commenced immediately.

Waking up is the process of looking deeply into your real condition, and allowing the Holy Spirit to take you into all those areas in your life which contradict the pattern of Jesus.

Remembering, in Sardis's case, was looking back over its history and realizing how laziness and neglect had allowed the enemy to invade the citadel while warnings went unheeded. It meant scrutinizing the reasons why the decay had set in and the causes for the corruption which had become open hypocrisy and pretence.

Repentance is the word *metanoia*, which means a change of mind and heart, allowing the will and motivation to be turned against former sin and neglect, and towards the regenerating power of the Holy Spirit.

Obedience is seeing the will of God set forth clearly before your eyes, and planting your feet firmly on the path of subservience to the Lord of the Church, the One who distributes the gifts and energies of the sevenfold Spirit, and who holds the seven stars in his right hand (3:1).

All this applies to churches as well as to believers, because our doctrinal dogmatisms as well as our insensitive shepherding can manifest deadness and corruption as much as do our neglect and spiritual inertness.

Religious people can do insensitive and cruel things, affirming their nasty religion by a denial of their humanity. People have been tortured and burned at the stake for unorthodox doctrine, and others have been rejected for unmarried pregnancies or as victims of AIDS. As Jesus foresaw:

They will put you out of the synagogues. Indeed an hour is coming when those who kill you will think that by doing so they are offering worship to God (John 16:2).

The warning of Christ indicates his judgement – the lampstand of the Church may be removed, the name erased from the Book of Life. There are yet areas of spiritual life which remain but they are ready to die. If the Sardis folk do not wake up, remember the past, repent of sin and neglect, and obey the will of God, then judgement will overtake them suddenly – like a thief in the night (3:3). This reflects the gospel warning in Matthew 24:42, and the apostolic warning in 2 Peter 3:10. This trail of scripture speaks of the suddenness of judgement, the surprise of retribution, the need to wake up to the perilous situation.

The time is critical, judgement is imminent, but all is not lost, and Christ, in spite of such powerful warning, patiently gives counsel, lovingly expects response, and faithfully stands waiting to impart the gifts of his Holy Spirit to those who will hear.

*

Prayer

Christ our Mediator and Advocate:

You know us through and through, and knowing, you continue to love, and long to save us from our hypocrisy and neglect;

Stir us up to a new awareness of our need; tune our ears to listen clearly; melt our hearts to follow obediently; make our will wholly yours;

Then shall our vision be renewed, our lives made over, and your divine patience be rewarded. Amen.

*

Response

Ask two or three of your non-Christian friends their opinion of your local church, of the churches in your neighbourhood, and of the wider Church of God and its influence in the world.

Share these findings with your Christian group and make them a matter of prayer and action.

*

Day 5 Evening
The Faithful Few

All is not lost. There are a faithful few who have not been lured away by the heathen rites of paganism, nor been dragged down by the torpor of a moribund church. Even in a dead church, if it remains a church at all, the scriptures and the memoirs of the apostles are read, and the sacrament of the eucharist is celebrated. There are those whose hearts respond and whom God is preparing as a remnant to become salt, light and leaven to the lethargic majority who are under judgement unless they repent.

God always has his remnant, and it is often through the small, faithful group or the lone prophet who speaks and lives the truth that the majority is stirred up, repentance is kindled and revival takes flame. It was by the remnant army of just three hundred men that Gideon miraculously defeated the Midianites (Judges 7); it was when Elijah was despairing to death that he was the only one left that God assured him that there were seven thousand others who had not bowed to or kissed the god Baal – a remnant (1 Kings 19:18). And smaller still, although David had gathered the army around him, there were just three mighty men who crept into the enemy camp of the Philistines by night to draw water to satisfy the thirst of his yearning (1 Chronicles 11:17–19).

Perhaps Jesus remembered these three faithful ones when he took Peter, James and John with him to watch and pray in the Garden of Gethsemane, as his watchful remnant, but in their case they fell asleep with sorrow and grief (Matthew 26:

36–46). Christ could say of the church at Sardis as he said sorrowfully of them: 'Could you not stay awake with me one hour? Stay awake and pray that you may not come into the time of trial' (vv.40f.).

If you belong to a church like Sardis at all, then strive to be among the faithful few, for to them Christ speaks words of encouragement with great promise. Before I entered The Society of St Francis I lived with The Community of the Transfiguration, near Edinburgh. One of the brothers was the missionary bishop Neil Russell, for whom I had a great admiration. One day he discovered that I had previously had pastoral charge of a church in Resolven, South Wales, which was called Sardis. He commented: 'They must have been very brave and honest to call themselves by that name.' They were, and are – and that is the point of a faithful remnant – they are honest, transparent people of integrity.

I have been guiding the reading of some of the novices, and yesterday Nicholas and I were commenting on Gerard Hughes' *God of Surprises*, noting this very quality of transparent honesty and integrity. He is writing for 'bewildered, confused or disillusioned Christians, who have a love-hate relationship with the Church to which they belong, or once belonged', and he writes:

I am a Catholic, a priest and a Jesuit. Many people still think that Catholic priests, perhaps Jesuits especially, never suffer confusion, bewilderment or disillusion. I do.

I used to think such negative feelings were a sign of failure which I must overcome, or at least ignore if I were to remain a Jesuit priest. Now I realize how wrong I was, for God is the God of surprises who, in the darkness and the tears of things, breaks down our false images and securities. This in-breaking can feel to us like disintegration, but it is the disintegration of the ear of wheat: if it does not die to bring new life, it shrivels away on its own.

There is a price to pay living as the faithful few in a moribund church, and it is these faithful ones who undergo the pruning process by which God sanctifies them in order that they may produce fruit in the midst of barrenness and infertility.

Here it is that the promises of Christ become operative. To those who follow him faithfully and humbly in obedience, Christ promises that they will walk with him in the white garments of truth and integrity, and their names shall shine in the Book of Life as Christ confesses their names before the Father, as they have confessed him in the world.

It is through this faithful remnant that Christ will revive and renew his apostasizing and lethargic church, and when the Church is renewed and pulsating again with spiritual life, then the world will see the difference, the neighbourhood will feel the radiant warmth of genuine spirituality, and the Church will no longer have to bolster an empty reputation.

The Book of Life is known to God alone. It is not synonymous with the church membership roll, and names cannot be entered by subscription, merit, worldly popularity or reputation. It is the number of those who seek to dwell within the love of God, and who have responded to his call down the ages. It contains the names of those who have been baptized into the fellowship of Christ's Church and who live by faith. But it is even wider than that, for it is the roll call of the kingdom of God.

In ancient cities the names of citizens were recorded until

death, then they were effaced from the Book of the Living. This is the idea behind Exodus 32:32 and Psalm 69:28, where to be erased or blotted out simply means physical death.

In the New Testament the dimension of eternity is added, for when the disciples return from a successful mission of teaching and healing, Jesus says to them:

Nevertheless, do not rejoice at this, that the spirits submit to you, but rejoice that your names are written in heaven (Luke 10:20).

Paul rejoices that his fellow workers' names are inscribed in the Book of Life (Philippians 4:2), and the promise of future hope which Christ communicates to the faithful remnant in Sardis is caught up in the enrolled saints in glory:

You have come to Mount Zion and to the city of the living God, the heavenly Jerusalem, and to innumerable angels in festal gathering, and to the assembly of the firstborn who are enrolled in heaven, and to God the judge of all, and to the spirits of the righteous made perfect, and to Jesus, the mediator of a new covenant (Hebrews 12:22–24).

So when the Risen Christ makes his promise to that small but faithful remnant in the decadent city and church of Sardis, in that tiny part of the Roman empire at the end of the first century, he lifts their eyes and their hearts to an eternal inheritance laid up for those who overcome by faith. They shall walk with him in white, their names shall shine in the Book of Life, and they shall be part of the eternal song which is sung before the angels of heaven and before the Eternal Father.

*

Prayer

Lord Jesus, King of Glory:

In the darkness of our world your light forever shines;

In the midst of apostasy, denial and lethargy you preserve a faithful remnant;

Save us from our sins, deliver us from apostasy, sustain us in the midst of lethargy and decadence;

Revive our drooping spirits and set us among the remnant who faithfully proclaim your truth by words and deeds, in life and in death;

To your eternal praise and glory.   Amen.

*

Response

1. Write a letter from the Risen Christ to your own church indicating:
   a) signs of life
   b) signs of decay
   c) the necessary remedy, however radical
   d) the possible consequences in the neighbourhood
2. Write a similar letter from the Risen Christ to yourself, along the same lines.
3. Invite a friend to do the same. Then write such a letter to each other, as from the Risen Christ, and compare all the results prayerfully.
4. Ask yourselves: Can all this be carried further?

*

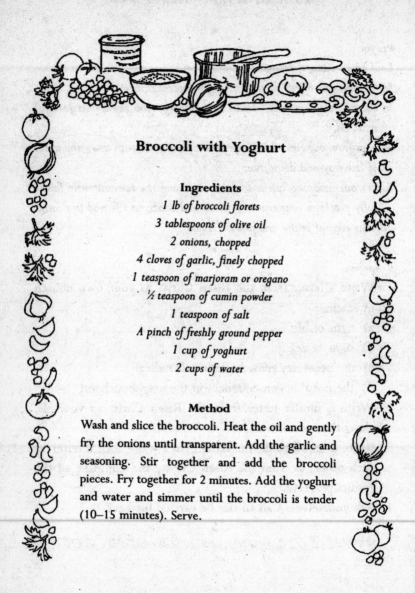

Broccoli with Yoghurt

Ingredients

1 lb of broccoli florets
3 tablespoons of olive oil
2 onions, chopped
4 cloves of garlic, finely chopped
1 teaspoon of marjoram or oregano
½ teaspoon of cumin powder
1 teaspoon of salt
A pinch of freshly ground pepper
1 cup of yoghurt
2 cups of water

Method

Wash and slice the broccoli. Heat the oil and gently fry the onions until transparent. Add the garlic and seasoning. Stir together and add the broccoli pieces. Fry together for 2 minutes. Add the yoghurt and water and simmer until the broccoli is tender (10–15 minutes). Serve.

I have set before you an open door

Philadelphia

Letter to the Church at Philadelphia
Revelation 3:7–13

And to the angel of the church in Philadelphia write:

These are the words of the holy one, the true one, who has the key of David, who opens and no one will shut, who shuts and no one opens.

I know your works. Look. I have set before you an open door, which no one is able to shut. I know that you have but little power, and yet you have kept my word and have not denied my name. I will make those of the synagogue of Satan, who say that they are Jews and are not, but are lying — I will make them come and bow down before your feet, and they will learn that I have loved you.

Because you have kept my word of patient endurance, I will keep you from the hour of trial that is coming on the whole world to test the inhabitants of the earth.

I am coming soon; hold fast to what you have, so that no one may seize your crown.

If you conquer, I will make you a pillar in the temple of my God, you will never go out of it.

I will write on you the name of my God, and the name of the city of my God, the new Jerusalem that comes down from my God out of heaven, and my own new name.

Let anyone who has an ear listen to what the Spirit is saying to the churches.

Day Six

Love and Faithfulness: The Church at Philadelphia

Philadelphia lies about thirty miles south-east of Sardis, on the road to Laodicea. It owes its name to Attulus, king of Pergamum 159–138 BC. His love for his brother earned him the name Philadelphos, for that is its meaning, and it calls to mind the inclusive rendering of Psalm 133:1: 'How very good and pleasant it is when kindred live together in unity!' It is appropriate that I am writing these words on the Sunday of Christian Unity Week, and the hymn I sang at morning prayer was Charles Wesley's 'Christ from Whom all blessings flow', containing the stanzas:

Gently may we all agree,
  Touched with loving sympathy:
Kindly for each other care;
  Every member feel its share.

Love, like death, has all destroyed,
  Rendered all distinctions void;
Names and sects and parties fall:
  You, O Christ, are all in all.

It is appropriate, too, that this church received only words of praise and commendation from Christ, and with such a name and such a reputation it was the ideal missionary church, for how can a church be the vehicle of God's love unless the members love one another?

The city was actually founded for a missionary purpose, being situated where the borders of Mysia, Lydia and Phrygia met, so that it could function as the open door of opportunity to spread Greek language and culture.

So Christ speaks of the new open door of evangelistic opportunity (3:8), bearing the best news of all − that the true meaning of Philadelphia is that God is the loving Father, and that therefore love is at the centre of human life for those whose lives are open to Christ.

Philadelphia was decimated by the same earthquake which destroyed Sardis in AD 17, and was similarly given aid by the emperor Tiberius. In gratitude it took the name Neocaesarea − the new city of Caesar, but that reverted to Philadelphia in emperor Nero's time. The new name that Christ promised (3:12) was one which would never fail, for it had the ring of immortality and the new and eternal city of God.

Although the people reacted courageously under the earthquake, and rebuilt the city, yet it continued to suffer fearful tremors which caused frequent panic, the people running from the city into the open country. Perhaps that is why Christ promised that they would never need to run out of the eternal city (3:12f.).

Philadelphia was not the equal of Ephesus or even Laodicea, and for law courts its citizens had to go to Sardis. Yet it has survived all three, and continues on the same site. In later times it resisted the growing power of the Turks, as Ramsay points out:

> It displayed all the noble qualities of endurance, truth and steadfastness which are attributed to it in the letter of St John, amid the ever-threatening danger of Turkish attack; and its story rouses even Gibbon to admiration.

It stood until the period AD 1379–90 when the united Byzantine and Turkish forces brought it down. But even after that it continued its Christian witness in the midst of Islam, remaining a place of Philadelphia, of love and faithfulness.

Day 6 Morning
An Open Door

Immediately, in our text, we are faced with the One who is holy, who is true, and who has the key of David. This means that the Christ who is united to our humanity in his incarnation is also separated by the holiness which manifests the being of God (Isaiah 40:25; 43:15).

He is also true in the sense of being himself the Truth, the basis of all reality, the guarantor of all that is good and true and beautiful. He is one with us in our humanity, and one with the Father in his divinity, so those human and divine qualities are to be reflected in his Church. And that Church, in its local manifestation, is the *ecclesia*, called out, and separate from the sinfulness of the world – and yet immersed in the humanity which God loves and redeems.

The local church at Philadelphia lived up to its name, and was holy in life and true in character. At the same time it was a human and loving missionary church, ready to be a channel and instrument of the saving will of God.

Christ, in our test, holds the key – the only key which can open up the secret meaning of our lives, the door of opportunity and the gate of blessing. It is also the symbol of ultimate authority over life and death. Listen to that opening description again:

Do not be afraid; I am the first and the last, and the living one. I was dead, and see, I am alive forever and ever; and I have the keys of Death and of Hades (1:17f.).

Because of such a revelation, the little power of the Philadelphian believers is swallowed up in the power of the living Christ, and they need never ultimately be afraid again.

Already he tells them that they have not denied his name, and warns them of the hour of trial that will soon break upon them (3:10). He does not tell them that they will not be harmed, neither does he promise that they will survive physically. Indeed he tells them to hold fast so that no one shall seize their crown. This means that though fears and tribulations may surround them, and though persecution may become seven times hotter in the conflict, yet Christ has the keys of death and hell, and the crown of victory is before them. Whatever the earthly conflict their souls are ultimately in the hands of Christ.

So this door which Christ places before the Philadelphian believers is not only a door of opportunity and a door of evangelistic endeavour, but a door which opens upon earth and leads to the coming kingdom. They are encouraged to take every evangelistic opportunity which is offered to them, to invite the surrounding heathen and Jewish people to enter through the door of salvation which is Christ (John 10:9). But they are also encouraged not to be afraid, for in the midst of persecution the door of the kingdom is wide open to them and no one is able to shut it.

The Apocalypse follows the rest of the New Testament in stressing that God does not promise deliverance *from* persecution, but deliverance *in* it. Those who hang on to physical life will lose it, and those who relinquish it for the sake of their Saviour will keep it to eternal life (John 12:25).

This is the vision set before the Christians persecuted under the emperor Domitian in these seven letters, but the whole

Apocalypse was written for the very purpose of setting such persecution in the context of the almighty power of God, who at last will bring his persecuted, exiled and pilgrim people home in victory and glory:

> One of the elders addressed me, saying, 'Who are these, robed in white, and where have they come from?' I said to him, 'Sir, you are the one that knows.' Then he said to me, 'These are they who have come out of the great ordeal; they have washed their robes and made them white in the blood of the Lamb.
>
> For this reason they are before the throne of God, and worship him day and night within his temple, and the one who is seated on the throne will shelter them. They will hunger no more, and thirst no more; the sun will not strike them, nor any scorching heat; for the Lamb at the centre of the throne will be their shepherd, and he will guide them to springs of the water of life, and God will wipe away every tear from their eyes' (Revelation 7:13–17).

Our present world is no different, for suffering in the name of Christ, and suffering for peace and justice, takes place on an even wider scale. But the same promises hold good.

In our own part of the world, with our parochial vision, we may feel that the edge is not so keen, that the cultural conscience has been influenced by our Christian heritage – but there are subtler enemies. The reason why we are not overtly persecuted may well be because we have so compromised the truth that we are no longer a threat to an economic capitalism. Or even that we are part of it and participate in the sale of arms and military hardware, trusting in our coveted nuclear arsenal, and polluting our world. Wendell Berry in an article,

'What We Learned from the Gulf War', written in 1991, made a devastating criticism:

> *We must recognize that the standards of the industrial economy lead inevitably to war against humans just as they lead inevitably to war against nature. We must learn to prefer quality over quantity, service over profit, neighbourliness over competition, people and other creatures over machines, health over wealth, a democratic prosperity over centralized wealth and power, economic health over 'economic growth' ... If we want to be at peace, we will have to waste less, spend less, use less, want less, need less. The most alarming sign of the state of our society now is that our leaders have the courage to sacrifice the lives of our young people in war, but have not the courage to tell us that we must be less greedy and less wasteful.*

This may sound like a far cry from Christ's word to the Christians in Philadelphia, but as we reflect upon their situation in a hostile and persecuting Roman empire, and our situation in a greedy, polluting and violent world, we realize that the enemies are those who deface and pollute the image of God in his creatures and in his creation.

It is our duty and privilege, as it was theirs, to live and proclaim gospel values, to live and die for the way of Christ, to stand against violent people and ideologies, armed only with the compassion of Christ and the boldness of the Holy Spirit.

The Philadelphian church had little power, but faith in a great God. And he promised never to let them down.

*

Prayer

Lord Jesus, Keeper of the Keys:

You open and close the doors of opportunity, of witness and of eternal life;

Grant that when you open the door we may cross its threshold, and when you close the door we may wait in patience.

You have called us to be holy and true in a world of duplicity and violence; grant that proclaiming the missionary news of your salvation, and living lives of simplicity, joy and gentleness, we may be able to lead others through the door which is the gateway to eternal life;

So we shall be among those who love one another, and who live by your grace. Amen.

*

Response

In a quiet place reflect upon your life and the many doors of possibility and opportunity which God has placed before you.

Write down the names of such doors, marked talents, gifts, training, blessings, witness, friendships, etc.

How many doors have you walked through positively, and how many have you failed to enter? Think of the blessings which followed or the possibilities lost.

Ask the Lord to show you another door, another possibility, another opportunity, and for the grace to push it open if he turns the key.

*

Day 6 Evening
'I have loved you ... I will keep you'

This evening we shall reflect upon the attitude of Christ to his people, and their attitude to their persecutors and neighbours. If we take parts of the Apocalypse in isolation from the rest of the New Testament canon, or make much of Christ's role as judge and fail to give primacy to Christ as Saviour and Redeemer, we shall find ourselves in grave error. And errors of belief translate into attitudes and lifestyles which perpetuate the wrong emphasis.

It is the case that God is angry with those who perpetrate acts of injustice and cruelty, as it is clear that Christ confronts all manner of unloving, especially in the guise of religious hypocrisy. But God does not act as an irate schoolmaster or a vengeful tyrant – and he does not lose his temper!

Retribution is not an end in itself, but leads to correction and salvation, and those who persist, finally, in the rejection of the divine Love choose their own ultimate hell of annihilation. That is why we have to be careful about the symbols and images of the book of Revelation, for its true message is salvation and the victory of love, when all that opposes the reconciling Gospel will fall into the pit it has dug for itself – for God will not coerce or impose salvation. The final word of the Apocalypse is the word grace, and in the consummation of all things, when all powers in heaven and on earth are put under the authority of Christ the Redeemer, then he will surrender all things to the Father, so that God may be all in all (1 Corinthians 15:26).

We affirm all this in the context of the church at Philadelphia, the name of which indicates the love which exists within the fellowship of believers, and under the banner upon which is written: 'I have loved you ... I will keep you' (3:9f.).

One problem that confronts us here is that, as in the letter to Smyrna, the Jews are spoken of as agents of persecution, and we have noted in the story of Polycarp that it was the Jews who first sent up the persecuting cry, and who even broke the sabbath in order to carry fuel for the fire of martyrdom. Does the recording of this smack of anti-Semitism, and if so, how are we to deal with it?

Our text speaks of the synagogue of Satan, of Jews who are lying, and of their coming to bow down before the feet of the Christians in Philadelphia.

In the Old Testament, the term 'synagogue of the Lord' is the Greek rendering of 'assembly of the Lord' (cf. Numbers 2:4). The Jews at Philadelphia, instead of recognizing in Jesus the Saviour and Messiah who would bring all their deepest hopes and yearnings to fruition, not only rejected him, but persecuted his church – 'he came to what was his own, and his own people did not accept him' (John 1:11).

So the promise of the Gentiles coming to bow at the feet of the Jews (Isaiah 45:14) has been reversed. The 'new Israel' has been grafted into the covenant, and those who are Jews in name only, and to whom the promises were originally made, have made themselves into the enemies of God.

Well then! Is the Church of God, as the new Israel, to turn about and reject God's ancient people, or does the fact that the Messiah himself is the Jew *par excellence* mean that he yearns for their salvation and reconciliation? The task of the Philadelphian believers is not to return evil for evil, but to learn the way of Christ.

Certainly the protomartyr Stephen revealed the Gospel's power of reconciliation and compassion when he cried out, as the Jews were stoning him to death: 'Lord, do not hold this sin against them' (Acts 7:60). This was an overflow of the forgiving love of his Lord who prayed, as he was being crucified: 'Father, forgive them; for they do not know what they are doing' (Luke 23:34).

How difficult it is for us to look truth full in the face, to confront the realities of persecution, intolerance, cruelty and exclusivism, and not only to forgive, but to extend a hand of friendship on the basis, not of agreed opinions, but of our common humanity, for we are all born in the image of God.

It is necessary, for truth's sake, to read history objectively, to confess with sorrow that there have been such things as Islamic jihad, Jewish holy war and Christian crusade. Indeed, the fall of Philadelphia itself, after centuries of Christian witness, was brought about by the betrayal of fellow Christians, for the united forces of the Byzantine emperor Manuel II and the Turkish sultan Bayezid I, destroyed Christian churches in Asia Minor.

Whatever the horrors of the past or the difficulties of the present, we cannot go on, as members of the great world faiths, persecuting and slaying one another. Not only is this far from the will and purpose of the Prince of Peace, but it is humanly reprehensible and will only confirm the suspicions of many good humanists and ethical atheists that religion itself is the source of exclusivisms, bloodshed and interreligious and international persecution. We may point to the fact that the great tyrants of the twentieth century were Hitler and Stalin, who massacred many millions in the names of Fascism and Marxism, but that does not lessen our responsibility.

So it is that in the text before us, we have a church in which Christians are persecuted by Jews, and in the course of history both will be overrun by the Turks — a racial, national and religious ferment in which peaceful coexistence and co-operation should have been the outcome, but where instead religion became combative ideology, and racial pluralism gave way to tensions and hatred.

We could be writing about our own situation in the contemporary world, mirrored in the assassination of Yitzhak Rabin by an Israeli Zionist. Yet there are moments of hope even at such times, for King Hussein of Jordan wept at Rabin's funeral.

There have often been times and places where Muslims, Jews and Christians have lived together as neighbours and friends — and there must be again. One of the Christian theologians who has been working in this area is Hans Küng. He has recently founded the Global Ethic Foundation, and he describes the task with clarity when he says that there can be no peace among the nations without peace among the religions; that there can be no peace among the religions without dialogue between the religions; that there can be no dialogue between the religions without investigation of the foundation of the religions.

Such a task can only be taken up in a spirit of openness. It is a door of opportunity set before us, and only Christ holds the key. He speaks words of judgement to false Jews and false Christians. In the middle of the letter he says: 'I have loved you … I will keep you,' and this is the pattern for believers, to follow the way of Christ, who 'when he was abused, he did not return abuse,' when he suffered, he did not threaten; but he entrusted himself to the one who judges justly' (1 Peter 2:23).

Now a positive word to those who overcome. They will be made pillars in the temple of God. There was a custom in Asia Minor that when a priest died after faithfully serving the temple to which he was attached, he was honoured by the erection of a pillar upon which his name was inscribed. There is no temple in the New Jerusalem at the end of the book (21:22), so this is a spiritual pillar which implies strength and durability in the worship and adoration of God. As pillars were sometimes sculpted and inscribed, so God's name, and Christ's mark, will be set upon the believer (3:12).

James, Peter and John were strong apostolic pillars in the Church of God (Galatians 2:9), but this promise to the believers in Philadelphia is thrown wide open to all who trust in the strength and grace of Christ to overcome.

There are three names to be given to the overcomer in verse 12, and they encapsulate the whole meaning of a life surrendered to God. They are:

* the name of God who created the believer to bear his image and share his likeness;
* the name of 'Jerusalem above' which is the society of the redeemed to sound forth the gospel call of love throughout creation;
* the name of Christ, which is the name of Redeemer and Saviour, who will at last put down all sin, and present the whole creation to the Father.

When this reaches its consummation, the days of persecution, suffering and death will be ended, for in some of the final words of the prophecy God says:

> *See, the home of God is among mortals.*
> *He will dwell with them and be their God;*
> *they will be his peoples,*
> *and God himself will be with them;*
> *he will wipe every tear from their eyes.*
> *Death will be no more;*
> *mourning and crying and pain will be no more,*
> *for the first things have passed away (21:3f.).*

*

Prayer

Lord Jesus, King of the nations:

When will the kingdoms of this world become the kingdom of your love?

When shall all crying and suffering cease, and human wickedness come to an end?

Enable us to become true followers of the way of peace; in being abused may we not abuse in return; shape us into that community of forgiveness and reconciliation whose strength is in gentleness;

None of these things are possible without you, so grant us the anointing of your Holy Spirit.   Amen.

*

Response

Consider what is, at best, the goal of the great world faiths. Is there any excuse or reason for human beings, let alone religious people, to engage in persecution and hatred?

What is the place of Christ as Saviour and Reconciler in a world of violence and suffering?

What glimpses of hope and encouragement can you see, and how are you involved in bringing about greater harmony and understanding? *Philadelphia* implies shared love within the church fellowship. Is that a mark of your church?

Bearing in mind Hans Küng's counsel above, will you take steps towards simple friendship and sharing with people of other faiths in your neighbourhood, with perhaps a visit to synagogue, mosque or temple?

*

Vegetable Fritters with Greek Mayonnaise

Ingredients

For the batter

1 cup of flour
1 teaspoon of salt
A pinch of ground pepper
¾–1 cup of warm water
1 egg, beaten
1 tablespoon of olive oil

For the fritters

1 potato
1 aubergine, sliced
2 courgettes, sliced
2 firm tomatoes, sliced
1 green pepper, sliced
Olive oil for frying

Method

Make up batter by sifting flour with salt and pepper. Make a well in the middle and add the water, stirring in gradually until smooth, then mix in egg and olive oil. The mixture should make a creamy batter. Leave it to stand while you prepare vegetables. Boil potato until almost soft (about 15 minutes), and slice. Heat some oil in frying pan. Stir the batter and dip the vegetable slices in it, then fry them. When golden, remove and drain on absorbent paper. Serve with Greek Mayonnaise.

Greek Mayonnaise

Beat together 1 egg, pinch of mustard powder, pinch of salt, 2 tablespoons of lemon juice, 1 tablespoon of dried herbs, 4 tablespoons of olive oil.

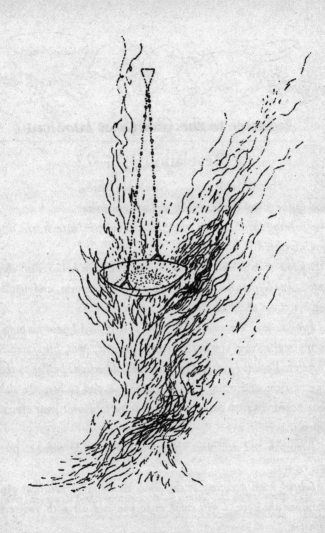

Buy from Me gold refined by fire

Laodicea

Letter to the Church at Laodicea

Revelation 3:14–22

And to the angel of the church in Laodicea write:

The words of the Amen, the faithful and true witness, the origin of God's creation:

I know your works; you are neither cold nor hot. I wish that you were either cold or hot. So, because you are lukewarm, and neither cold nor hot, I am about to spit you out of my mouth.

For you say, 'I am rich, I have prospered, and I need nothing.' You do not realize that you are wretched, pitiable, poor, blind and naked. Therefore I counsel you to buy from me gold refined by fire so that you may be rich; and white robes to clothe you and to keep the shame of your nakedness from being seen; and salve to anoint your eyes so that you may see.

I reprove and discipline those whom I love. Be earnest, therefore, and repent.

Listen! I am standing at the door, knocking; if you hear my voice and open the door, I will come in to you and eat with you, and you with me.

To the one who conquers I will give a place with me on my throne, just as I myself conquered and sat down with my Father on his throne.

Let anyone who has an ear listen to what the Spirit is saying to the churches.

Day Seven

Tepid and Nauseous: The Church at Laodicea

Laodicea, on the river Lycus, is the seventh and last in our circuit of churches, some forty miles south-east of Philadelphia. It was founded by Antiochus II (261–246 BC), and named after his wife Laodice. Situated in the Lycus valley, three roads converged on Laodicea. The main road from the east entered by its Ephesian gate and left by its Syrian gate. This was the great road of commerce, the same one Ignatius travelled on his way to martyrdom in Rome.

The Roman peace enabled the city to become prosperous, so that it became a banking and financial centre, famous for its manufacture of clothes, and the site of a medical school.

The church was probably founded by Epaphras of Colossae (Colossians 4:12f.), and St Paul wrote to the Laodicean church. The letter to the Ephesians also was sent to Laodicea. Colossae was situated ten miles east and Hierapolis six miles north, on the north bank of the Lycus.

There was a very large Jewish population in the city, and since every male Jew paid two drachmae temple tax, a great deal of currency went to Jerusalem every year. In 62 BC the governor, Flaccus, became alarmed at the amount and put an embargo on the export of currency. From the amounts involved it has been estimated that there were at least 7,500 male Jews in the district.

The Jews were not only wealthy but influential, for in Heliopolis a 'Congregation of Jews' existed which had authority to levy and retain fines, and there was an archive office for storing Jewish legal documents.

Much of the background of Laodicea is picked up in the text of the letter as we shall see, and this is indicated in the words of A.M. Ramsay:

> Laodicea was a small city until after the Roman period had begun; then it rapidly became great and rich. Destroyed by an earthquake in AD 60, it disdained to seek help from the liberality of the emperor as many of the greatest cities of Asia had done. Hence its boast, Revelation 3:17, 'I am rich and have gotten riches, and have need of nothing.' It was renowned for the beautiful glossy black wool of its sheep, and carried on a great trade in garments manufactured from this wool. Owing to its central position at the point where the great trade route from the East was joined by several branch roads ... it became a centre of banking and financial transactions. Hence, Revelation 3:18, 'I counsel thee (not to take the gold of thy bankers, but) to buy of me gold refined by fire, and (not the glossy black garments made in the city, but) white garments.'

Day 7 Morning
The Judging Christ

This was the church of which nothing good could be said. Or we may say that it was not good enough to be called good and not bad enough to be called bad.

If we think of the angel of the church as the bishop or pastor, then this person may well have been Archippus, for there is a tradition which affirms it. He may well have been the son of Philemon the wealthy convert of Colossae (Philemon 2). It is said that he became the first bishop of the neighbouring Laodicea, but may have lacked the zeal and discernment necessary for his task, calling forth salutary words from Paul after his reference to Laodicea in Colossians 4:17: 'Say to Archippus, "See that you complete the task that you have received in the Lord."' This was thirty years or so before the Apocalypse was written, but here are the beginnings of a degeneration which comes to light clearly and publicly in this letter, and of which Christ is the judge.

Christ as Judge is neither his primary nor his consummatory role. He is first and last Saviour and Lord, and the news that he brings is of forgiveness, healing and salvation to a lost and needy world. It also has to be said that his judgement is towards repentance and restoration – it has to do with correction and chastisement. But it is nevertheless searching and searing judgement.

We shall come to the shining radiance of his tenderness and patience before we are finished, but we must, in this letter and in our lives, be confronted by the One who tells us the truth with penetrating honesty and integrity. That is why he is called 'the Amen, the faithful and true witness' (3:14). The Hebrew of Isaiah 65:16 speaks of *the God of Amen*, and here this name is given to Christ. The word *Amen* is the guarantee of truth and fidelity, and this is carried into Jesus' frequent statements: 'Amen, Amen I say to you' (John 1:51; 3:3, 5, 11).

Christ's authority is further affirmed in that he is 'the origin (*arche*) of God's creation' – the Author, the Source, the One by whom all things came into being (John 1:13).

We have noted that there is immense comfort when Christ says, 'I know ...' to some of the churches. But here he exposes the vulnerable spot, the nauseating religion which was professed in Laodicea: 'I know your works; you are neither cold nor hot ... so because you are lukewarm, and neither cold nor hot, I am about to spit you out of my mouth.' The NRSV, following most of the modern translations, is not as crude as the text could/should be, for the verb *emeo* should be translated *to vomit*, and is the root from which our word *emetic* is derived! Such a church is to be utterly rejected, and its lampstand removed from its place (2:5).

We may imagine the Christians gathered on the Lord's Day for their eucharist, with a certain flurry of excitement because of the letter from John of Patmos which is to be read. Following fast upon the opening words, this divine estimation of their state before God is made clear, and also the steps they must take before this judgement of ejection is carried out.

There is nothing like personal experience to illustrate unpalliative truths. In my mind is my allergy to mushrooms; the very thought of them makes me feel queasy, and I remember a farmhouse casserole which (accidentally) included mushrooms, on a mission when I was to preach at Brecon Cathedral that evening. A little while after the meal I suspected that they were among the ingredients, and then I was violently sick for two hours until I had got rid of the whole meal! Not a nice description (or experience). Perhaps the Laodiceans thought of the nauseous, tepid mineral springs up the road in Hierapolis – and they understood.

Christ continues:

You say, 'I am rich, I have prospered, and I need nothing.' You do not realize that you are wretched, pitiable, poor, blind and naked (3:17).

It was the proud boast of Laodicea that in the devastating earthquake about AD 60, unlike Ephesus and Sardis, the rich and independent citizens of the city refused Roman help – they had need of nothing.

How easily we become obsessed and influenced by our culture; self-satisfied so that our spirituality keeps in line with our smug lifestyle. Laodicea had to learn that it could not gain admittance to the kingdom of God because it was a banking centre. The prosperous clothing trade due to the violet-black glossy wool of their sheep did not prevent them from appearing naked in the sight of God. Also, the famous Phrygian eye-salve of its medical school did not prevent their spiritual blindness, lacking in the basic spiritual discernment of their own poverty, nakedness and pitiable wretched state. What could be done?

Therefore I counsel you to buy from me gold refined by fire so that you may be rich; and white robes to clothe you and to keep

> *the shame of your nakedness from being seen; and salve to anoint*
> *your eyes so that you may see (3:18).*

How could they buy? Only with the refined currency of faith (1 Peter 1:7), and only with a humble and contrite heart (Isaiah 57:15). How could their nakedness be covered? Only with the new white robe of righteousness and restoration, as the prodigal son learned when he returned to his father (Luke 15:22). How could spiritual discernment and vision be restored? Only with the divine eye-salve that Jesus gave to the blind man at Siloam (John 9:6ff.), so that they can see their precarious state. As a result of this they would then be enabled to look to Jesus as the Physician who diagnoses their condition, and as the one who prescribes the remedy which is contained in his own forgiving and renewing love.

As part of the diagnosis we have to reflect upon the words *hot*, *lukewarm* and *cold*. We may take it that *hot* is the state of a church or a believer set aflame with the zeal of the Holy Spirit, consumed with the love of Christ, and longing to share it with others. The Wesley brothers encapsulated this meaning in their lives and writings – take the first stanza of a hymn by brother Charles:

> *O Thou who camest from above*
> *The pure, celestial fire to impart,*
> *Kindle a flame of sacred love*
> *On the mean altar of my heart.*

Cold may well mean a group or a person untouched by the Gospel, who have never heard, never understood, never been moved by the grace of the Holy Spirit, and therefore who are, as yet, unresponsive to the call of Christ.

Lukewarm indicates that beginnings had been made, there had been a response to the call, a light within the soul, a kindling warmth of the heart and mind. But now it has died down, lost fervour, allowed zeal, concern and enthusiasm to abate because other things have taken central place – and spiritual lukewarmness is the result.

The outward trappings are still there, services are held, scripture read, psalms sung, eucharist celebrated – but the heart has gone out of it all, the fire is nearly extinguished, the lamp of God is just about flickering out in the temple of God (1 Samuel 3:3). 'These people honour me with their lips, while their hearts are far from me' (Isaiah 29:13).

Such people can be likened to the seed sown among thorns, for the concerns of the world and the lure of wealth choke the seed and it yields nothing (Matthew 13:22). The King James Version is much more literal and explicit than the new translations: 'So then because thou art lukewarm, and neither cold nor hot, I will spue thee out of my mouth' (3:16). And the state of such people as a result is spelled out in the dire words of 2 Peter 2:21f.:

For it would have been better for them never to have known the way of righteousness than, after knowing it, to turn back from the holy commandment that was passed on to them. It has happened to them according to the true proverb, 'The dog turns back to its own vomit,' and, 'The sow is washed only to wallow in the mud.'

153

There is more hope for the *cold* prostitutes and tax collectors than for the *lukewarm* Pharisees to enter the kingdom of God (Matthew 21:31). So there is more hope for an unconverted sinner than for the man or woman who, having once been moved to response by the Gospel, has now lapsed into a state of self-satisfied, indolent smugness.

Then suddenly a new note is sounded. It is not a reversal or even a change of direction, but a continuation of the stern rebuke, yet gently making clear that the Judge is also the Saviour, that the rebuke and discipline is that of a lover who is jealous for the beloved. Christ does not speak of the punishment of sinners but of the correction and guidance of those who are the objects of his tender affection: 'I reprove and discipline those whom I love. Be earnest, therefore, and repent' (3:19).

Can we hope that there were those among the lukewarm Laodiceans who were first of all scared, then awakened, touched, moved and brought to a new sense of repentance and faith, so that the flame of love was kindled again and began to burn in hope? These may have been a few, perhaps a remnant like the group in Sardis, but from such a small company a living witness could arise again in Laodicea, like the phoenix rising from the ashes.

What such a group would discover in actual experience is that the Christ whose face was set against them in judgement was actually the Saviour who loved, who yearned, who wept for them in their lukewarm indifference to him. And in turning back to him they would find such amazing joy in tears of repentance, and such an infilling of his holy and life-giving Spirit, that they would wax warm, and hot, in zeal and love. As William

Cowper put it: 'Behind a frowning providence he hides a smiling face.'

Cowper was taught a theology of damnation for the non-elect which preyed upon his frail psyche. He suffered depression, and there were times when he was plunged into the darkness of judgement when he suspected that he was not among the elect. John Newton, the converted slave driver, was a friend of his, and one of the things that Newton suggested was that they write hymns together – which later became the Olney hymns. This was a means of healing for Cowper, for as he penned poetry and wrote hymns light began to dawn, and moments of simple grace and love welled up within him. One of the hymns in which the judgement of God is seen to melt into tenderness, and which illustrates the point we have been making, begins 'God moves in a mysterious way'. Two of the stanzas run:

> You fearful saints, fresh courage take,
> The clouds you so much dread
> Are big with mercy, and shall break
> In blessings on your head.

> Judge not the Lord by feeble sense,
> But trust him for his grace;
> Behind a frowning providence
> He hides a smiling face.

This is the transformation we see in our text, and we shall consider it this evening.

*

Prayer

You see us, Lord Jesus, in our helplessness,

Labouring for the gold that perishes,

Shoddy in the garments of our own making,

Seeing so much without discernment or vision.

Have mercy upon our arrogance and hypocrisy, dear Lord;

Deliver us from the uncontrolled flame of dogmatic zeal, and from the
   flickering wick, ready to die;

Grant us the quiet, steady flame kindled by your Spirit,

A flame of love towards you, a flame of witness towards the world,

That we may become again a church of the living God.   Amen.

*

Response

Imagine you are a member of the Laodicean church, hearing this letter for the first time. As you examine your individual and church life you see that Christ's evaluation is on the ball.

How would you go about setting your own life right? How would you, if you had influence with the leadership, go about setting the church's sights right?

What about your influence as Christian and church, upon the world around you?

Are there political ideologies which need Christian comment? Are there practical tasks in local council, school and social life which call for your pair of hands?

Can you link with Christian/humanitarian groups to bring about change for good in the lives of people in poverty, fear or minority exclusion?

Will you do it?

*

Day 7 Evening
Patient, Waiting Saviour

The book of Revelation is the only apocalyptic writing we have in the New Testament. This kind of writing is addressed to a crisis situation of emergency and therefore contains suffering, warning, conflict and judgement. There are dire threats about falling short, encouragements to heroic witness and expectations of martyrdom. There is much about evil and demonic powers and the wicked works of evil people, with angelic powers of light and darkness as the context and backdrop of the whole drama.

From the beginning of chapter four, the book of Revelation launches into this whole area, and for this reason many people, from earliest times, have questioned its place in the canon of the New Testament. Apart from an acknowledgement of its entry into the canon in the early Church, it is of special interest that the two great Reformers Luther and Zwingli both rejected it, and it seems to be the only New Testament book on which Calvin produced no commentary.

The lesson to be learned from this is that this book is a devotional treasure house, which in times of great conflict and persecution has proved itself to be God's word to the persecuted and an immense source of strength, yet great care must be taken in the interpretation of its prophecies. There is a kind of fundamentalist mind-set which delights in such interpretations, not only changing metaphorical and analogical language into literal and historical fact, but also setting dates and times which the rest of scripture forbids us to do (Matthew 24:36; Acts 1:7).

157

A preoccupation with such prophetic literalism and demonic conflict shifts the centre of what the Gospel and the New Testament are actually about. The centre of the Gospel is mystical union with Christ, the lover with the beloved, the mystery of 'Christ in you, the hope of glory' (Colossians 1:27). This is unfolded on a personal and a corporate level of the believer and the Church – and that Church is seen as light in a dark world.

In our text, we have come to the place where our attention is brought back to the loving centre, where judgement turns to tenderness, and where the divine heartbeat of love is felt even in this church of Laodicea which, of itself, possesses no redeeming feature. At the core of the counsel, the warning and judgement of Christ is the Face of Love. 'Listen,' he says, 'I am standing at the door, knocking ...', calling to mind words of the yearning lover:

> My lover put his hand to the door,
> and I was thrilled that he was near.
> I was ready to let him come in.
> ... I grasped the handle of the door,
> I opened the door for my lover,
> but he had already gone.
> How I wanted to hear his voice!
> I looked for him, but couldn't find him;
> I called to him, but heard no answer.
> (Song of Solomon 5:4–6; GNB)

We have to ask ourselves what kind of invitation this is. Christ is portrayed not only outside his Church, but the words become personal – he is outside the heart of the individual believer. This is one place where the use of inclusive language makes the text ambiguous. The Greek text is in the singular, addressed to each person in the Laodicean church, for the church cannot be renewed unless individuals experience a change of heart. Look at it again:

> Listen! I am standing at the door, knocking; if you hear my voice and open the door, I will come in to you and eat with you, and you with me (3:20).

These words to the Church and to the believer have a threefold significance. They have a Gospel meaning, a Mystic meaning and an Eschatological meaning. Let's look at each in turn.

First, the gospel meaning. In Keble College, Oxford, and in St Paul's Cathedral, London, hang the 'two originals' of *The Light of the World* by Holman Hunt. It is a somewhat sentimental picture but much loved by ordinary people, and has been the means of drawing many people closer to the love of God.

It is a gospel picture, showing Christ the Saviour standing, knocking patiently, at the heart-door of one who has allowed the entrance to become tangled with weeds and brambles. Christ is crowned, but with thorns, he bears the lantern which symbolizes his word, his garments are both prophetic and priestly, and he waits ...

I learned to love this picture before I was taught that it was not a 'good painting', and I am glad, for the Lord uses many means to reach our hearts. I write these words on 25 January, the commemoration of the conversion of St Paul. It was on this day, at twelve years of age, that I came to Christ in a simple, childlike way, and with tears opened my heart and life to him.

I simply 'opened the door', for the handle is on the inside, and I was enabled to open it by the gracious influence of the Holy Spirit. As I told one of our novices this week, Christ has been more real to me since that day than even those I have dearly loved in the world. The invitation contained in our text is addressed to the reader, and the simple, childlike question is: 'Have you opened your heart to Jesus as Saviour and Lord?'

Second, there is the mystical meaning. We have already noted it in the words from the Song of Solomon (sometimes called the Song of Songs). It means that Christ may be acknowledged as Saviour, with personal and corporate commitment in church and daily life, but there is no flame, no rapture of love, no contemplative dimension of prayer, no realization of union with God in Christ that the great saints and mystics have experienced. One of the poems of Christina Rossetti reveals the mystical centre of the disciple John's communion with Christ, and it encapsulates this mystical dimension:

> My Lord, my Love! in pleasant pain
>   How often have I said,
> 'Blessèd that John who on Thy breast
>   Laid down his head.'
> It was that contact all divine
>   Transformed him from above,
> And made him amongst men the man
>   To show forth holy love.

Yet shall I envy blessèd John?
  Nay not so verily,
Now that Thou, Lord, both Man and God,
  Dost dwell in me:
Upbuilding with Thy Manhood's might
  My frail humanity;
Yea, Thy Divinehood pouring forth,
  In fullness filling me.

Now that Thy life lives in my soul
  And sways and warms it through,
I scarce seem lesser than the world,
  Thy temple too.
O God, who dwellest in my heart,
  My God who fillest me,
The broad immensity itself
  Hath not encompassed Thee.

Third, there is the eschatological meaning. Eschatology has to do with the 'last things', and this apocalyptic book of Revelation is certainly speaking of persecution and suffering in that vein. The church at Laodicea is in real trouble, for Christ stands outside the door, and the danger is that the church's lampstand may be removed and the day of grace will have ended. The words of our text remind us of Luke 12:35f.:

> *Have your lamps lit; be like those who are waiting for their master to return from the wedding banquet, so that they may open the door for him as soon as he comes and knocks.*

If the Revelation affirms anything, it is that the Christ of God who became incarnate as the Saviour Jesus in Bethlehem will one day come again in glory for the consummation of all things. And however one views eschatology and judgement, it will be a disclosure of joy and rejoicing for those who look for him, but a time of fear and loss for those who have rejected him.

He is patient, tender, and longing to enter into every church, every human heart, but he will not forcibly break down barriers. And it is not that he comes to judge. He comes to save. It is we who judge ourselves, for the 'knocking' becomes fainter as we neglect or reject it, so that we hear it no longer, and we fritter away our day of grace.

The earliest epistles reveal a situation where the coming of Christ was expected at any moment, so that even domestic life was subjected to his imminent return. The later epistles realized that the time scale was longer, for 'with the Lord one day is like a thousand years, and a thousand years are like one day' (2 Peter 3:8), but the fact of Christ's coming was not in doubt. The Church has continued to confess its belief in Christ's second coming, in which the whole of creation will be caught up in God's ultimate purpose for our world (Romans 8:18–25).

Finally, in our text there are the consequences of opening the door to Christ. There is the gracious entrance which transforms both the church and the human heart; there is the fellowship of love symbolized in the eucharistic meal of Christ's body and blood; there is the sharing of Christ's throne symbolizing mystical union with Christ and participation in the life of the Holy Trinity.

Is it not strange that the letter which begins with the sharpest rebuke, the sternest warning of judgement and the most devastating diagnosis of a moribund condition, is the one which reveals the divine Love most tenderly, with the invitation to forgiveness, reconciliation, mystical union and ultimate salvation in the day of Christ's appearing?

It is the revelation of God's inmost heart, the good news that his judgement is contained within his love, and that it is not his will that any should perish, but that all should come to repentance and salvation at the last (2 Peter 3:9).

*

Prayer

Lord Jesus, Light of the World:

Your word of judgement leads to your heart of mercy, and your counsel of holiness leads to your tender love;

If you stand at the door of the Church and at the door of our hearts today, enable us to hear your patient knocking;

Grant that the door may be opened wide in repentance, in yearning, in welcome.

If we do not heed your invitation of peace, then our hearts will remain restless, but if you enter you will bring healing and joy for the present, and life and light forever in the world to come.   Amen.

*

Response

Consider ways in which, with each rejection of love, the human heart may become less responsive, less tender, less sensitive to human suffering and need.

Apply such thinking to yourself in relation to Christ, and then in relation to your family, friends, neighbours, and to political and ecological dimensions.

Perhaps you know someone whose heart and conscience have become desensitized by experiences of rejection in love, or because of being wounded, they have built up a wall of protection.

Could it be your task, in prayer and love, gently to breach the wall, to open up the heart, and to be the instrument of Christ's patient love? Apply all this to relations between the churches, and to hope for unity within the wider Church of God.

*

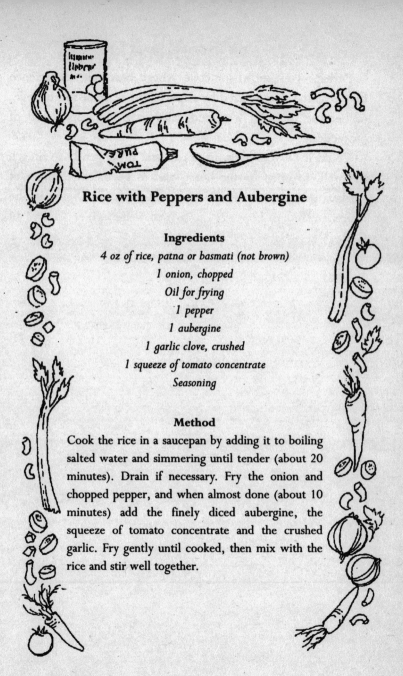

Rice with Peppers and Aubergine

Ingredients

4 oz of rice, patna or basmati (not brown)
1 onion, chopped
Oil for frying
1 pepper
1 aubergine
1 garlic clove, crushed
1 squeeze of tomato concentrate
Seasoning

Method

Cook the rice in a saucepan by adding it to boiling salted water and simmering until tender (about 20 minutes). Drain if necessary. Fry the onion and chopped pepper, and when almost done (about 10 minutes) add the finely diced aubergine, the squeeze of tomato concentrate and the crushed garlic. Fry gently until cooked, then mix with the rice and stir well together.

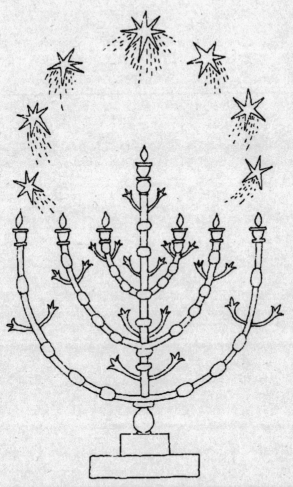

The Seven Churches: Earthly and Heavenly

Epilogue

THE LISTENING HEART

The task is complete, the prophecy sealed and sent with the messengers to the mainland of Asia Minor, and St John the Divine sits on the rocky projection of Patmos, gazing out into the heaving restlessness of the Aegean Sea.

It is as if the tumult and shouting of the Day of Judgement is over, sentence has been passed, wickedness is silenced and the righteous have entered into peace.

As the thudding repetition of the waves reverberates in the caves of Patmos, so the quiet murmur of the voice of Christ, the sound of many waters, whispers in John's heart, and all is at rest.

I have been preparing to write these closing words in the context of listening to the Opening and Adagio movements of Elgar's Cello Concerto. The sad and wistful beauty of Jacqueline du Pré's solo cello carries resolution, harmony and peace. My saturation in the Apocalypse of John over the last months has brought me to this place of resolution, consummation and rest, in which sin has been atoned for, judgement is contained in the everlasting mercy, and the whole creation flows back into the divine Love from which it took its rise.

There are periods in our human experience when the Lord allows us to enter into the strange peace of resolution and consummation as a foretaste of the life to come, though first we have to be plunged into the harrowing hell of conflict, cruelty and the warring of darkness against light. It can be joyfully affirmed that the Faith of Christ is no dualist religion in which eternal conflict, rebellion and evil continue for ever.

However dark the battlefield, whatever sins and evils have beset people and nations within and without, there comes the time at last when Love is seen to be at the heart of things, and its victory is manifest because it is of the essence and nature of God.

There can be no easy or simplistic resolution. Only those who have entered into the experience of the exceeding sinfulness of sin, and who have measured, with Christ, the blood and sweat of Gethsemane and the cry of dereliction from the Cross, can begin to plumb the depths of the divine compassion. But it has to be affirmed and maintained against all comers – the victory remains with Love.

The profoundest truths are rooted into our human experience, and the dying and rising of Christ is part of the human-divine pattern. I recall one fearful episode which happened to me in my third year of solitude, when I lived in a freezing caravan, in December, 1992. It began with a sudden night awakening, accompanied by swinging, intermittent bouts of vertigo, with high temperature and sudden rise of blood pressure.

I've just looked at my journal of that period, and read up the passage of that awful week of dizziness, lack of balance and physical control. When the whole thing abated, I felt as if I had entered into a harbour of rest after a violent storm at sea, in which my frail boat had been tossed at the mercy of the waves.

There were times, as I record, when the only position which freed me from the sudden invasion of dizziness and vertigo was kneeling upright on my prayer stool, repeating the variation of the *Jesus Prayer*:

> Lord Jesus Christ,
> Son of God,
> Let Your healing flow down
> Upon me.

And I recall now the sense of immense gratitude and peace which followed the episode, because it was a balm to my soul, a resolution of the conflict and an entering into rest. And this is the analogy which has been pressed upon me as we emerge from the deep waters of judgement and mercy with which we have been dealing in the book of the Revelation.

Thus John sits on the rocky shore and contemplates, with listening heart, the vistas of eternity. He has been carried through earthly restlessness and persecuting darkness, into the heavenly dimension of tranquillity and light. We have shared some of his journey, conscious that the Holy Spirit has been speaking to us in the words of the Risen Christ.

The One who stands in the midst of the seven earthly lampstands is he who sustains his Church during its tribulation and suffering. The One who holds the seven stars in his right hand is he who transforms the Church militant on earth into the Church triumphant in heaven.

The evolving question which sounds in our listening heart at the end of this journey concerns the person of Christ. It is a question for the sevenfold Church, and it comes to us in a personal and threefold form:

- Do I know him?
- Do I love him?
- Do I yearn for him?

It is only as the Church and the believer affirm this progressive pilgrimage that the will and compassion of Christ will be imaged in our lives and in our world. And in the affirmation of this threefold question we shall ultimately arrive at the end of the journey, which is the beginning of eternity, in some of the final words of the Apocalypse:

Then the angel showed me the river of the water of life, bright as crystal, flowing from the throne of God and of the Lamb through the middle of the street of the city. On either side of the river, is the tree of life with its twelve kinds of fruit, producing its fruit each month; and the leaves of the tree are for the healing of the nations.

Nothing accursed will be found there any more. But the throne of God and of the Lamb will be in it, and his servants will worship him; they will see his face, and his name will be on their foreheads.

And there will be no more night; they need no light of lamp or sun, for the Lord God will be their light, and they will reign forever and ever (Revelation 22:1–5).

The Way of Love

Following Christ Through Lent to Easter

Brother Ramon SSF

The Way of Love will take you on a personal pilgrimage from Shrove Tuesday when – in the traditional worship of the Christian Church – 'the alleluias cease', to Easter Sunday with its explosive celebration of the Risen Lord.

This forty-eight-day journey invites you to follow in Christ's footsteps through the Gospels to the dramatic events of the first Easter. Each day there is an opportunity to stop and reflect, to find strength and wisdom for our larger journey in the world and to discover in our own experience the road that leads through suffering and death to abundant new life.

Designed for individual or group use, *The Way of Love* will enrich understanding, nourish faith and draw us into closer union with the love of God which is the goal of all our journeyings.

The Heart of Prayer

Finding a time, a place and a way to pray

Brother Ramon SSF

Prayer is at the very core of our Christian faith, yet how many of us have said, 'I don't have time', or 'I don't know where to begin', or, even, 'I don't know how to pray'? The stresses of today's world make it increasingly difficult to set aside time to be still with God, and yet it is only through prayer that we can cope with the challenges of daily living and grow as individuals.

With refreshing simplicity, Brother Ramon tackles head-on the practical difficulties of nurturing a life prayer. From step-by-step instructions on how to create a place for prayer in your home, to advice on what to do when prayer seems a fruitless exercise, *The Heart of Prayer* will gently guide you into a deeper, more enriching experience of prayer.

'Honest and down to earth, but neither evasive nor sentimental, this book will appeal to Christians of differing backgrounds ... there is a gentleness about his writing that inspires trust and co-operation.'

Life and Work (Record of the Church of Scotland)

Laughter, Silence and Shouting

An anthology of women's prayers

Compiled by Kathy Keay

Laughter, Silence and Shouting is a wide-ranging anthology of prayers that articulate women's deepest longings, fears, joys and dreams. Included are prayers by Mother Teresa, Florence Nightingale, Emily Brontë, Helen Keller, Janet Morley, Teresa of Avila and Julian of Norwich.

Ranging in origin from the Celtic tradition to modern-day feminist theologians, these prayers offer gentle spiritual guidance and introspection for women everywhere. Over 160 prayers are presented in categories such as 'Our Daily Lives', 'Relationships', 'Work', 'Illness', 'Grief', 'Daring to Believe', 'Stages of Life', and many more.

This beautiful book is the perfect gift for reflection and meditation, and provides a useful resource for women the world over.

'... eloquent, honest and full of vitality.'

The Universe

Dancing On Mountains

An anthology of women's spiritual writings

Compiled by Kathy Keay

'I have named this anthology *Dancing On Mountains*, for in the midst of life's demands, there are always moments to celebrate; historic and often incidental moments of break-through, breathtaking, inspiring and energizing, when the Spirit enlivens the commonplace, making us want to dance.'

Kathy Keay

Dancing On Mountains is a collection of writings by women of all ages, times, conditions and countries, expressing their spirituality through their everyday lives and through the unbridled possibilities of their dreams. Including selections from Emily Brontë, Helen Keller and Emily Dickinson, as well as many previously unknown writers, each passage in *Dancing On Mountains* reflects a voice which will inspire, encourage and comfort readers on their own journey through life.

After reading English at Oxford, Kathy Keay worked as a free-lance writer, editor and journalist, giving workshops and seminars in the UK, the USA, India, Africa and South Africa. Kathy was a prolific writer, with nine published titles to her credit. She died in December 1994, after a long fight against cancer.

Celtic Daily Prayer

From the Northumbria Community

The ancient and beautiful tradition of daily prayer finds new expression in this collection of readings and simple liturgies which are shaped by Celtic spirituality.

Various complines for morning, midday and evening prayers are included here, together with an Order for Holy Communion and a Family Shabbat. An inspirational selection of readings for every day of the year will ensure that *Celtic Daily Prayer* becomes a prayer book to use again and again.

'... it opens another treasure trove for those who seek to widen their spiritual life and give a structure to their own prayer. The choice of reading is wide and reflective, simple in its approach, direct in its message ... another enriching gift to the whole Church.'

The Way

Celtic Night Prayer

From the Northumbria Community

> Each light, each dark
> Be near me,
> Uphold me.

When night closes in, we have to look at things differently. There are many sorts of night – the long nights of winter time, nights of difficulty or unanswered questions, times of loneliness and the apparent absence of God.

There is also the warmth of time spent with friends, the happy tiredness at the end of the day, the joy of the bridal night or thanksgiving at an evening meal.

The Celtic understanding welcomes and celebrates the presence of Christ in all of these. The candle in the window burns. *Celtic Night Prayer* contains readings for every day of the year, together with daily complines based on the lives of the Celtic saints and liturgies for baptisms, weddings, times of difficulty, bereavement and festivals.

Glory Under Your Feet

From transfiguration to transformation

Michael Marshall

In the story of the Transfiguration, Jesus gives his disciples a powerful glimpse of what men and women can become when they are restored to the heart of God. Charged with a vision of the glory which is our inheritance in Christ, the disciples were empowered to bring his healing and light into the pain and darkness of the world.

Christ still calls his disciples to transform society but only a transfigured church – one which seeks after and experiences God's glory – can accomplish this. *Glory Under Your Feet* offers six meditations on the Transfiguration which challenge us to enter more fully into the life of worship, wonder and adoration, and to proclaim to creation at large that 'the whole world is full of his glory' (Isaiah 6:3).

The Gaze of Love

Meditations on Art

Sister Wendy Beckett

Sister Wendy Beckett invites us to leave the limitations of what we already know and discover the infinities of a deeper vision communicated to us through art. Art, like prayer, is always an expression of longing, and modern art – with its striking and unfamiliar forms – offers one of the most exhilarating and adventurous routes we can follow to that world of freedom, love and beauty which lies behind all our longings.

Sister Wendy has selected forty works of art, mostly contemporary, and her illuminating commentaries on each of them provide an excellent companion on what is an unforgettable journey of discovery.

Sister Wendy Beckett is a Carmelite nun living in a hermitage in rural Norfolk. She has thrown open the world of art appreciation for millions of viewers in her popular BBC TV series, *Sister Wendy's Odyssey*, *Sister Wendy's Grand Tour* and *The Story of Painting*.

The Mystery of Love

Saints in art through the centuries

Sister Wendy Beckett

Following her enormously successful book, *The Gaze of Love*, Sister Wendy Beckett now shares her profound knowledge and insights in to the portrayal of the saints in art through the centuries with her characteristic simplicity and joy.

For most of us, saints are remote figures – unreal, inaccessible, detached from the farrago of normal life. Through this selection of some of the world's most exquisite paintings from the thirteenth century to the present day, Sister Wendy helps us to discover that holiness is a way of life open to all. More to do with attitude than attainment, sanctity is within everyone's grasp.

The Mystery of Love explores the spiritual terrain of classic and contemporary art and promises a truly individual experience for every reader.